S0-BQX-877

BARRON'S BOOK NOTES

HOMER'S

The Iliad

BY

George Loutro

SERIES EDITOR

Michael Spring
Editor, *Literary Cavalcade*
Scholastic Inc.

BARRON'S

BARRON'S EDUCATIONAL SERIES, INC.
Woodbury, New York / London / Toronto / Sydney

ACKNOWLEDGMENTS

We would like to acknowledge the many painstaking hours of work Holly Hughes and Thomas F. Hirsch have devoted to making the *Book Notes* series a success.

© Copyright 1984 by Barron's Educational Series, Inc.

All inquiries should be addressed to:
Barron's Educational Series, Inc.
113 Crossways Park Drive
Woodbury, New York 11797

Library of Congress Catalog Card No. 84-18499

International Standard Book No. 0-8120-3421-X

Library of Congress Cataloging in Publication Data

Homer's the Iliad.

(Barron's book notes)
Summary: A guide to reading "The Iliad" with a critical and appreciative mind. Includes background on the author's life and times, sample tests, term paper suggestions, and a reading list.
1. Homer. Iliad. [1. Homer. Iliad. 2. Classical literature—History and criticism] I. Title.
PA4037.Z5S55 1984   883'.01   84-18499
ISBN 0-8120-3421-X (pbk.)

PRINTED IN THE UNITED STATES OF AMERICA

456   550   987654321

CONTENTS

ADVISORY BOARD

We wish to thank the following educators who helped us focus our *Book Notes* series to meet student needs and critiqued our manuscripts to provide quality materials.

Murray Bromberg, Principal
Wang High School of Queens, Holliswood, New York

Sandra Dunn, English Teacher
Hempstead High School, Hempstead, New York

Lawrence J. Epstein, Associate Professor of English
Suffolk County Community College, Selden, New York

Leonard Gardner, Lecturer, English Department
State University of New York at Stony Brook

Beverly A. Haley, Member, Advisory Committee
National Council of Teachers of English Student
Guide Series, Fort Morgan, Colorado

Elaine C. Johnson, English Teacher
Tamalpais Union High School District
Mill Valley, California

Marvin J. LaHood, Professor of English
State University of New York College at Buffalo

Robert Lecker, Associate Professor of English
McGill University, Montréal, Québec, Canada

David E. Manly, Professor of Educational Studies
State University of New York College at Geneseo

Bruce Miller, Associate Professor of Education
State University of New York at Buffalo

Frank O'Hare, Professor of English
Ohio State University, Columbus, Ohio

Faith Z. Schullstrom, Member, Executive Committee
National Council of Teachers of English
Director of Curriculum and Instruction
Guilderland Central School District, New York

Mattie C. Williams, Director, Bureau of Language Arts
Chicago Public Schools, Chicago, Illinois

HOW TO USE THIS BOOK

You have to know how to approach literature in order to get the most out of it. This *Barron's Book Notes* volume follows a plan based on methods used by some of the best students to read a work of literature.

Begin with the guide's section on the author's life and times. As you read, try to form a clear picture of the author's personality, circumstances, and motives for writing the work. This background usually will make it easier for you to hear the author's tone of voice, and follow where the author is heading.

Then go over the rest of the introductory material—such sections as those on the plot, characters, setting, themes, and style of the work. Underline, or write down in your notebook, particular things to watch for, such as contrasts between characters and repeated literary devices. At this point, you may want to develop a system of symbols to use in marking your text as you read. (Of course, you should only mark up a book you own, not one that belongs to another person or a school.) Perhaps you will want to use a different letter for each character's name, a different number for each major theme of the book, a different color for each important symbol or literary device. Be prepared to mark up the pages of your book as you read. Put your marks in the margins so you can find them again easily.

Now comes the moment you've been waiting for—the time to start reading the work of literature. You may want to put aside your *Barron's Book Notes* volume until you've read the work all the way through. Or you may want to alternate, reading the *Book Notes* analysis of each section as soon as you have finished reading the corresponding part of the original. Before you move on, reread crucial passages you don't fully understand. (Don't take this guide's analysis for granted—make up your own mind as to what the work means.)

Once you've finished the whole work of literature, you may want to review it right away, so you can firm up your ideas about what it means. You may want to leaf through the book concentrating on passages you marked in reference to one character or one theme. This is also a good time to reread the *Book Notes* introductory material, which pulls together insights on specific topics.

When it comes time to prepare for a test or to write a paper, you'll already have formed ideas about the work. You'll be able to go back through it, refreshing your memory as to the author's exact words and perspective, so that you can support your opinions with evidence drawn straight from the work. Patterns will emerge, and ideas will fall into place; your essay question or term paper will almost write itself. Give yourself a dry run with one of the sample tests in the guide. These tests present both multiple-choice and essay questions. An accompanying section gives answers to the multiple-choice questions as well as suggestions for writing the essays. If you have to select a term paper topic, you may choose one from the list of suggestions in this book. This guide also provides you with a reading list, to help you when you start research for a term paper, and a selection of provocative comments by critics, to spark your thinking before you write.

THE AUTHOR AND HIS TIMES

Homer's *Iliad* originated at the beginnings of Western civilization. Its power is so timeless that it has been read continuously for more than 2500 years. Yet its origin lies shrouded in mystery, tangled in mythology, religion, and ancient tribal history. Aside from these elements, the real excitement of the *Iliad* lies in its brilliant poetry, which is sustained for more than 15,000 lines, bringing an age of heroes and their exploits to life with clarity, complexity, and depth of feeling.

Homer has been known since classical Greek times as the author of the *Odyssey* and the *Iliad*—and that is about all that can be said for certain about him. The ancients regarded him as practically a god, equal to the muses (who were the divine inspiration for all arts). Facts about Homer the man have long been the subject of hot debate among scholars. *Perhaps* Homer also wrote a group of long poems, still called the *Homeric Hymns*. *Perhaps* Homer didn't actually write the two great epic poems but merely pieced together small sections written by many different poets over centuries. *Perhaps* there was no Homer at all, and the poems were a kind of oral history, written and recited by numerous poets and much later collected into the books we now know. Each of these theories has been offered as true, and each remains unproven.

What is certain is that the ancient Greek scholars and commentators were convinced that Homer was real and lived in the 9th or 8th century B.C. Modern scholars generally agree that the *Iliad* was composed around 725 B.C. (the earliest written versions we have are hundreds of years later than that, so there's plenty of room for conjecture). But though we don't have the earliest texts, the ancient Greeks did, and Homer was written about, discussed, and analyzed throughout the classical Greek period.

One of the key controversies among Homeric critics is whether Homer composed his poems orally or whether he actually wrote them down. We do know that Homer's poems were recited in later days, at festivals and ceremonial occasions, by professional singers called *rhapsodes*, who beat out the measure with rhythm staffs. (There is a similar poet/singer in the *Odyssey* who sings a poem about the Trojan War. He is an old man, and blind; that may be the source behind the legend that Homer himself was blind.) Whether or not Homer actually wrote down his poems, it now seems certain that the *Iliad* and the *Odyssey* are part of an ancient literary tradition of oral composition. The stories on which they are based had probably been sung aloud for hundreds of years, and recited and memorized by one generation of poets after another before Homer took them in hand. After all, in Homer's time, writing was used mostly for inventories and business transactions. Recitation was the accepted means of relating myth and history.

The *Iliad* was part of a group of ancient poems known as the Epic Cycle, which dealt with the history of the Trojan War and the events surrounding it. Homer probably had at his fingertips most of these stories and characters, ready-made. His genius lay in choosing to focus on the story of Achilleus and in bringing a tragic depth to the story of the battle for Troy. Homer was writing about events that took place four or five hundred years before his own time, events already enlarged by the glamor of the past.

However tall Achilleus and Hektor actually were, by Homer's time their size was legendary, rather like that of comic book superheroes. For the Greeks, these heroes represented the ideals on which their civilization was based. At the same time, they symbolized elements of the human psyche, with its yearning for nobility and honor.

The world of the *Iliad* is based on history but grows into metaphor: we must look beneath the facts to its deeper meaning. Archaeologists have indeed discovered the remains of a supposed Troy on the coast of Turkey and the majestic ruins of palaces and tombs in Mykenai on the plains of Greece. Through the lines of the *Iliad*, however, the Greeks and Trojans still live for us, echoing in the human imagination.

THE POEM

A Comparison of Translations

Over the centuries there have been many translations of Homer's two great epics, the *Iliad* and the *Odyssey*. While the translations of course differ, none is more accurate than another. Each translator's understanding of Homer is influenced by his own personality and the time in which he lived. Some translations are in verse, others in prose. The quotations in this guide are from Richmond Lattimore's prose version of the *Iliad* (Chicago: University of Chicago Press, 1951). This translation is easy for modern readers to understand and comes close to what Homer was saying.

It is interesting to compare the various translations. Here are four versions of some lines from Book II.

> Say, Virgins, seated round the Throne Divine,
> All-knowing Goddesses! immortal Nine!
> Since Earth's wide Regions, Heav'n's
>   unmeasur'd Height,
> And Hell's Abyss hide nothing from your sight,
> (We, wretched Mortals! lost in Doubts below,
> But guess by Rumour, and but boast we know)
> Oh say what Heroes, fir'd by Thirst of Fame,
> Or urg'd by Wrongs, to Troy's Destruction
>   Came?
> To count them all, demands a thousand
>   Tongues,
> A Throat of Brass, and Adamantine Lungs.
> Daughters of Jove assist! inspir'd by You
> The mighty labour dauntless I pursue:

What crowded Armies, from what Climes they
  bring,
Their Names, their Numbers, and their Chiefs I
  sing.

—Alexander Pope

Tell me now, ye Muses that dwell in the
mansions of Olympus—seeing that ye are
goddesses and are at hand and know all things,
but we hear only a rumour and know not
anything—who were the captains of the
Danaans and their lords. But the common sort
could I not number nor name, nay, not if ten
tongues were mine and ten mouths, and a voice
unwearied, and my heart of bronze within me,
did not the Muses of Olympus, daughters of
aegis-bearing Zeus, put into my mind all that
came to Ilios. So will I tell the captains of the
ships and all the ships in order.

—Lang, Leaf, and Myers

Tell me now, Muses, dwelling on Olympos,
as you are heavenly, and are everywhere,
and everything is known to you—while we
can only hear the tales and never know—
who were the Danaan lords and officers?
The rank and file I shall not name; I could not,
if I were gifted with ten tongues and voices
unfaltering, and a brazen heart within me,
unless the Muses, daughters of Olympian
Zeus beyond the stormcloud, could recall
all those who sailed for the campaign at Troy.
Let me name only the captains of contingents
and number all the ships.

—Robert Fitzgerald

Tell me now, you Muses who have your
homes on Olympos. For you, who are
goddesses, are there, and you know all things,
and we have heard only the rumour of it and
know nothing. Who then of those were the

chief men and the lords of the Danaans? I could
not tell over the multitude of them nor name
them, not if I had ten tongues and ten mouths,
not if I had a voice never to be broken and a
heart of bronze within me, not unless the Muses
of Olympia, daughters of Zeus of the aegis,
remembered all those who came beneath Ilion. I
will tell the lords of the ships, and the ships
numbers.

—*Richmond Lattimore*

The Plot

For nine years the Achaians have besieged Troy.
During one of their raids on a nearby town they take
as captives two women: Chryseis, daughter of Chryses, priest of Apollo, and Briseis. Chryseis is given to
King Agamemnon as a war prize; Briseis is allotted to
Achilleus. When Chryses the priest comes to the
Argive camp seeking to ransom his daughter, Agamemnon refuses. At Chryses' behest Apollo sends a
plague on the Achaians.

Achilleus calls an assembly of the army, and the
soothsayer Kalchas explains the anger of the god. He
says that to appease Apollo, Agamemnon must
return Chryseis to her father. A violent quarrel
ensues, and Agamemnon says if he is forced to give
up his prize he will take someone else's to replace her.
When Achilleus expresses outrage at this demand,
Agamemnon takes Briseis from him.

Furious at the public insult, Achilleus vows to
refrain from fighting until he feels he is once again

properly valued. To effect this, he prays to his mother, Thetis, to plead his case before Zeus so that the Trojans will have victories, showing how sorely Achilleus is missed. Zeus assents to the plan.

All the Achaian army is marshaled before us in its splendor, but to little avail. Things go badly for them in battle. A long day of fighting seesaws between the Trojans and the Argives. Hektor returns briefly to Troy and speaks to Helen and Paris, to his mother Hekabe, and to his wife Andromache, who brings along their child, Astyanax.

After more inconclusive fighting a truce is proposed, during which time the Achaians build up their defenses with a large ditch and a fortified wall.

The next day the Trojans press the Argives, camping on the plain of Troy within striking distance of the Argive ships. Sensing defeat, Agamemnon admits his mistakes and offers to return Briseis to Achilleus, along with numerous other gifts. An embassy is sent to Achilleus with the proposal, but Achilleus refuses. The depth of his anger and shame forces him to hold out.

Diomedes and Odysseus carry out a nighttime spying expedition, during which the unfortunate Trojan Dolon is captured and made to talk. The two warriors then raid the outskirts of the Trojan camp.

Though Agamemnon in particular fights bravely, he and all the other major Achaians except Aias are wounded and forced to retire temporarily from battle. They are vulnerable to attack, and Hektor leads the Trojans crashing through the wall to reach the ships and burn them. But Achilleus is watching as the ships are torched. Neither he nor his comrade Patroklos can endure the defeat. Patroklos dons Achilleus' armor to fight against the Trojans, hoping they will mistake him for Achilleus and be demoralized. Patroklos rouses the Achaian army, and the Trojans are swept back to their city walls. Finally Hektor meets Patroklos face to face. Unarmed and shaken by Apollo, Patroklos is an easy victim for Hektor's spear.

A furious battle over the body of the dead Patroklos follows. The fierce fighting swings back and forth. Though Hektor seizes the armor, the Achaians are able to rescue the body. Pressed hard by Hektor and his forces, the Achaians retreat to their ships. By then Achilleus has been brought the terrible news of the death of his friend. Enraged and brokenhearted, Achilleus turns his anger from Agamemnon to Hektor. Though Achilleus has no armor, his mere appearance on the battlefield sends the Trojans fleeing in terror. Hephaistos crafts a stupendous set of armor for him, and after calling an assembly in which he and Agamemnon make their peace, Achilleus dons his new armor and rages into battle. Virtually all the Trojans are slaughtered. Achilleus brings Hektor down, ties him to his chariot, and drags him through the dust back to the ships.

The Achaians solemnly and elaborately bury Patroklos, while Achilleus laments and continues to brutalize the corpse of Hektor. The gods decide it is time to end this situation, and through Zeus' efforts Priam is sent to the Achaian camp to ransom the body of his son. Achilleus and Priam weep together over their mutual losses; then Priam returns to Troy with the body of Hektor.

Within the city walls the Trojans formally mourn their slain hero. Andromache, Hekabe, and Helen lament his passing. Hektor is buried.

The Characters

THE ACHAIANS

Achilleus (Achilles)

Achilleus, the son of Peleus and the sea goddess Thetis, is the leader of the Myrmidon contingent in the Trojan War. He is clearly the greatest of the Achaian warriors, in the judgment of both friend and enemy. The very sight of him on the battlefield is enough to send the Trojans fleeing in terror. Part of this power comes from his divine connections (his mother, Thetis, is a goddess), part from divine favor (at crucial points Hera and Athene look out for him and help him). This may also be a way of telling us of the enormous personal resources Achilleus has at his command.

Achilleus' vast emotional and physical powers are not always at the service of clearheadedness. Though his initial anger at Agamemnon is based on a sense of moral justice, his rage transcends his sense of morality. His emotions motivate him more than his thoughts, for he holds onto his fury even after Agamemnon offers to return Briseis with an apology. At that point he is no longer operating for a principle of fairness but is playing out his anger and punishing his enemies. Unfortunately, his comrades must pay the price of his passions. Not until his friend Patroklos has been sacrificed does Achilleus realize he has held his position too long.

Yet he is a complex, vital man. There is little doubt that he is right in taking a stand against Agamemnon's arbitrary decisions. He is one of those people who will fight to the death for what they believe in. Though his anger is fierce and relentless, there is nevertheless something noble in it. His sheer intensity demands respect. Because he is the one character actually to undergo change, the *Iliad* is really his poem. He loses much along the way but finally tempers his anger and reaches out in a gesture of compassion and peace toward Priam. Achilleus is first in the line of great Greek tragic heroes: his power makes him a hero, and his human blindness makes him tragic.

Agamemnon

Although many of the Greek commanders are kings in their own right, Agamemnon as commander-in-chief is king of them all, the "lord of men." We don't know whether he was given this position by virtue of the size or wealth of his home city, Mykenai, or because he is the powerful brother of the wronged Menelaos, or if he was voted as leader by all the other Achaians. Agamemnon's position, however, is the key to his character. Behind his actions in his quarrel with Achilleus lies a need to protect the trappings of his office, his rank. Quite simply, the king cannot have less than his subjects; respect must be shown. Yet Agamemnon, too, is rash, and there is pride in his actions as much as in Achilleus'. Though in battle he proves himself a strong fighter, he seems to be less sure as a leader. Several times he suggests that the Achaians give up their struggle, and an uncertainty about his position may make him too quick to jump at Achilleus. He is fast to recognize his wrong and make an apology (within the limits of his sense of rank), and shows a tender care for his brother, Menelaos. He seems to have genuine concern for his army; yet his judgment is none too sharp and he waffles. For all his kingliness, he is somewhat more bureaucratic than noble. His arbitrariness with Achilleus brings the heroic code into question.

Aias (Ajax)

Son of Telamon (hence called Telemonian Aias), he is, after Achilleus, the most imposing of the Argive warriors. He is frequently compared to a wall, and, in fact, as the last hero on the field after all the others have been wounded, he practically single-handedly defends the ships, roaming the fortified wall and then fighting from the prow of a boat. In a way, he is the Achaian defensive wall personified. He rarely speaks in council. What he does is defend his comrades to the end by sheer bulk and human will, and he does not give up until, the last man left, his very spear is hacked from his hands.

Diomedes

Diomedes is one of the great fighters for the Achaians. A true warrior, he supports Agamemnon when he feels the commander-in-chief is right and criticizes him when he is wrong. He is aided by Athene and is also responsible for wounding both Aphrodite and Ares—a remarkable feat for a mortal (although it is accomplished with the aid of Athene). He does not have Odysseus' spark of insight, but he speaks seriously, if haltingly. This may be because he is the youngest of the Achaian commanders. At times he seems too eager for battle, and his killing of Dolon has a touch of ruthlessness about it.

Menelaos (Menelaus)

The original husband of Helen, brother of Agamemnon, and king of Sparta, Menelaos has the unlucky distinction of being the person on whose behalf the war is being fought. He is dogged but not quite illustrious. He fights hard, though not particularly skillfully, and seems at times to be protected by Agamemnon. He is willing to bear the burden of responsibility but is not quite up to the challenge.

Nestor

Nestor, the aged king of Pylos, is one of the most elaborately conceived characters in the *Iliad*. He has not only a consistent set of ideas, but a consistent way of talking. He is forever long-winded and rambling. His characterization is due largely to his age: he is the oldest of the warriors at Troy. His wayward speeches are the product of a mind not quite as quick as it used to be, and also filled with a bit of blustery memory to pad the way. Yet he always has a point to make, and his age is not ridiculed. His experience gives him the justification to draw forth moral examples. That these examples come mostly from his own life shows a kind of fond respect for him on the part of Homer. Though no longer able to fight the way he used to, he is eager to aid the cause in whatever way he can.

Odysseus

Odysseus, king of Ithaca, is seen in many ways as the counterpart to Achilleus. He is the hero of the other epic by Homer, the *Odyssey*. Where Achilleus is passionate, Odysseus is resourceful. Achilleus is often seen as archaic man, the idealist, while Odysseus is viewed as modern man, the pragmatic survivor. In the *Iliad* he seems to have the quickest mind of all and is able to interrupt arguments with just the right measure of understanding and criticism. He always tries to keep things in order so that the matter at hand—the battle for Troy—can move forward. He is a great fighter and can be ruthless as well as tricky. He is also a true friend, the kind that does not mince words but tells you honestly (but with tact) what is the matter.

Patroklos (Patroclus)

Companion to Achilleus and son of Menoitios, Patroklos is the most sympathetic character in the *Iliad*. He is shown more often in friendship than in battle, and he is spoken of in the kindest terms by Achilleus and Briseis, both of whom he befriended. Though faithful to Achilleus, he can't endure the sight of his comrades being slaughtered, and if he can't rouse Achilleus to fight, he begs to be able to fight in Achilleus' place. The enormity of Achilleus' affection for him and the funeral rites held for his sake make him seem particularly noble.

THE TROJANS

Andromache

Andromache, wife of Hektor, is the most emotionally up-front character in the *Iliad*. Her speeches to Hektor are filled with passion and intensity. She is a devoted wife and mother and also shows her knowledge of the pleasure of emotional intimacy. Her grief is so directly communicated that she seems to stand for all Trojan women who have lost husbands and sons in the war. Her devotion and immediacy make us feel how much is wasted by the conflict at Troy, and add to our appreciation of Hektor.

Hekabe (Hecabe)

Wife of Priam and mother of Hektor, Hekabe incorporates the wisdom of women who understand intuitively the value of life. In urging Hektor not to go back into battle she reminds us of all the positive social aspects of existence. Her response to Priam's mission of reconciliation is similarly a primal concern: she has seen too much loveliness destroyed to trust anymore in the vicious war and its participants. She has a mother's instinctual protectiveness and rage, and says she would devour the liver of the hated Achilleus if she could—but her fury is born of grief and desperation.

Hektor (Hector)

Son of Priam and Hekabe, and husband to Andromache, Hektor is the most beloved and greatest fighter for the Trojans. Because the war is being fought at Troy, and Homer presents a picture of life within the city walls, we have a sense of Hektor as a domestic man as well as a fighter, which is unique in the *Iliad*. Though at times his fame as a fighter seems to outstrip his actual combat ability, he often single-handedly inspires the Trojan successes. By the time he crashes through the Achaian defensive wall, you could say he *stands for* the Trojan army. He can be impetuous and almost deluded in his fighting frenzy; he misreads omens and doesn't follow the advice of his comrades even when it's eminently worthwhile. Like Achilleus, he pursues his destiny with a single-minded force.

We sense that Hektor is not fighting a war he particularly believes in. He is quick to criticize Paris but is staking his life on defending Paris' actions. Hektor is the upholder of the heroic code *par excellence*. He understands that his city must stand or fall as one man. He defends its interests to the end for honor.

In his family relations Hektor exhibits sensitivity and sanity, a sharp contrast to his furious warring. He is courteous to Helen and devoted to Andromache. Though he tells his wife he must fight for the honor of the city, he also admits to her that her safety is his greatest worry—he would rather die than endure the sight of her made captive. He is tender and playful with his son, Astyanax, kissing him and actually laughing out loud—a rare occurrence in the *Iliad!*

While Achilleus seems somehow to stand above the Achaian cause and infuses the poem with his own tragic dimension, Hektor's tragedy is the tragedy of Troy. Though the gods admit he has always dutifully made his sacrifices to them, he gets embroiled in a web of fate that goes beyond his personal life. He is the "defender," and when he falls Troy falls. The burial of Hektor is the final act of the poem.

Helen

Even more so than Paris, Helen is the unwitting agent of Aphrodite. In her one important scene with the goddess she is literally forced to go to Paris against her wishes. Helen has a mysterious quality throughout the poem—as she will throughout Greek history—and her descent from Zeus (and Leda) may give her a special divine aura. Renowned for her beauty, she appears in the poem in flowing, sheer robes that only intensify her spectral quality. She frequently regrets her abduction by Paris and sometimes longingly thinks of her past with Menelaos. She furiously rebukes Paris for his cowardice, even expressing a wish that he die in battle so that she won't have to be with him any longer. By recognizing that Aphrodite has misled and used her, she also recognizes her own mistake. In the *Iliad*, Helen is a love goddess against her will.

Paris (Alexandros)

Pampered, beautiful, and slightly scandalous, Paris is the actual cause of the Trojan War—he stole Helen from his host, Menelaos. He is chided by Hektor for his womanizing and his prettiness, and even Helen seems to be fed up with his shamelessness and lack of modesty. He is an adequate fighter, but clearly his heart is somewhere else. While others are busying themselves with the gruesome realities of war, Paris is making love to Helen. Helen expresses regret but Paris never apologizes for bringing war down on his people and making them defend his rather indefensible actions. It is important to note that he achieves what he does through the aid and insistence of Aphrodite. He both benefits from and is *used* by her power.

Poulydamas (Polydamas)

Poulydamas, comrade of Hektor, embodies some of the spirit of both Patroklos and Odysseus, and fulfills a similar role as they do to Achilleus. He is the confidant of Hektor, and they seem to have had a long-standing relationship, but he is also clear-sighted when Hektor is impetuous, and the advice he gives—though not always followed—is careful and cleverly reasoned.

Priam

Priam is the Trojan counterpart to Nestor, the elder statesman and ruler with a dynasty. He is gentle and wise with his people, and is a fond (and prolific) father. Though his temper flares momentarily after the death of his son, Hektor, he treats even Helen respectfully. In his nighttime voyage to the Achaian camp he shows extreme courage. He is a man who cherishes his family and is able to reach out to Achilleus on this basis of human connections.

THE IMMORTALS

Just who or what the gods and goddesses are is one of the *Iliad*'s most intriguing questions. Sometimes they are religious figures, sometimes allegorical, sometimes psychological. Their relation to humans is extremely complex.

One way of looking at the gods is as a way of explaining how or why an event took place. Thus, if a warrior throws a spear at another warrior and misses, Homer might say that Athene caused the spear to overshoot its target. Similar to this approach is a psychological reading of the gods. When Helen is arguing with Aphrodite about going to Paris in Book III, we could say that's another way of Helen talking to herself and trying to figure out her true desire.

Sometimes the immortals in the *Iliad* can be seen as abstracted powers. Ares, for instance, is sometimes conceived of as war itself, not as a character. When the ground springs into bloom beneath Hera and Zeus in Book XIV, we could say that these two immortals themselves are possessed of the abstracted power of Aphrodite or, simply, love and fertility.

It is also clear that the gods and goddesses are *characters* in the *Iliad*, and as such display individuality and will in their actions. They are used as comic relief from the war, mimicking and mocking mortals. They are even parodies of humanity, and since they are supposedly so powerful (they're quite literally "above it all" on Olympos), their squabbles and tricks seem foolish in comparison. As characters, Homer uses the immortals skillfully to further his plot. They can intervene, favor one side or another, and force mortals to do things against their will. Though they can manipulate human lives, it is not at all clear that they can change human destiny. Thus, all their machinations may just be another way of saying this or that event took place. Comic or terrifying, they have this distinction in the poem—they are entirely creatures of the imagination. Unless, of course, they are real! . . .

Aphrodite

Goddess of love, Aphrodite fights in support of the Trojans, backing Paris in his judgment among the goddesses. She is not particularly successful in the battle and is wounded by Diomedes. She is not, however, all free and easy. She ruthlessly threatens Helen to do her bidding, and in a way the Trojan War is due to her manipulation. The power of love she governs is able to bring men to battle.

Apollo

The far-shooting god who causes the initial plague against the Achaians, Apollo is a defender of Troy and supporter of Hektor in battle.

Ares

Ares is the cold-blooded and bloodthirsty god of war. He aids the Trojan side and is sometimes pictured, allegorically, as war itself. Those who fight well are said to be "dear to Ares."

Athene (Athena)

Athene, in league with Hera against the Trojans—and for the same reason—is nevertheless more closely allied to Achilleus. Their relationship seems to be one of mutually powerful warriors. Athene, with her *aegis* that she shares with Zeus, is the most powerful war force of all. She is unflinching in combat, but her warrior stance is mediated by wisdom. She is the fiercest possible ally and is there for Achilleus at his most crucial moments.

Hephaistos (Hephaestus)

The lame god of the blacksmith's art (and its fire), Hephaistos fashions in his smithy a stupendous set of armor for Achilleus. Hephaistos can make himself a jester to amuse the other immortals but can also bring a fiercer power to bear. He sends a raging firestorm against the river Xanthos to aid Achilleus.

Hera

Hera, wife of Zeus, is one of the great troublemakers in the *Iliad*. Her anger and trickery keep things moving any time they threaten to go slack. She resents Zeus and his power as much as she may love him, but she has found ways of circumventing his will. She supports Achilleus chiefly because she loathes the Trojans—evidently because Paris insulted her by choosing Aphrodite as the loveliest of the immortals. She lies to both Zeus and Aphrodite to get her way, and her eye is that of a relentless housewife who does not miss a thing.

Poseidon

Poseidon is the god of the sea and is also known as the shaker-of-the-earth. He sides with the Achaians and bristles under the authority of his older brother, Zeus. He is extremely powerful, and when he commits himself to battle it feels as if the earth were coming apart.

Thetis

Divine mother of Achilleus, Thetis is emotional and devoted to her son. She pleads his case before Zeus and is ever-watchful from her domain in the sea. She knows of Achilleus' fated death and mourns him before he has actually died. As fiercely protective of her son as Hekabe is of Hektor, she arranges for Hephaistos to craft divine armor for Achilleus. In her sea caves she is surrounded by the company of the Nereids, the sporting sea nymphs.

Zeus

Zeus, the most powerful god of all—and quick to let everyone know it—is, in a way, the author of the poem. His plan to bring about the redemption of Achilleus really creates the plot structure. Zeus is the great sky god, one of the powerful second generation of Greek deities who took over the world from its primal forces. His father was Kronos, and his brothers are Poseidon and Hades. Among the immortals, his will is absolute; not absolute enough, however, to prevent him from being tricked by his wife Hera when she sets her mind to it. He has a fierce and merciless vengeance, and his will is crossed only at great peril. The face he shows to mortals is usually one of thunder and lightning, though he can also communicate via bird omens, usually in the form of an eagle. He tolerates the squabbles and feuds of the other gods and goddesses as if they were all his children. He demands—and rewards—absolute respect. He may or may not be able to influence fate, but he certainly has the scales in his possession.

Other Elements

SETTING

Historical Background

When the German archaeologist Heinrich Schliemann excavated the site of Mykenai in the late 19th century, he found amid an extraordinary series of royal graves a magnificent gold mask of a man. Schliemann announced to the world that he had gazed upon the face of Agamemnon, the "lord of men." Later scientific analyses proved that the mask predated Agamemnon by several generations, but nevertheless Schliemann's discoveries brought Homer's *Iliad* squarely into the real world. The historical reality of the Trojan War was established.

The thing that led Schliemann—as well as readers for several thousand years—to believe that Mykenai really existed was the vividness of Homer's descriptions. The world of the *Iliad* is filled with minute details of life in the Bronze Age. Even though most of Homer's information must have been handed down through centuries of memorized refrains, the pictures he presents often have the accuracy of documentary film. His descriptions of the bronze-armored Achaians, with their horse-plumed helmets, long spears, and figure-eight shields, give a picture of ancient Greek battle gear, which has since been proven accurate by archaeologists' discoveries. The detailed catalog of ships in Book II is practically a geography lesson, ranging over the entire Greek world. Today we still can walk around the foundations of the walled cities of Troy and Mykenai and see the remnants of the great-halled *megarons* and their battlements that Homer described. We can learn of weaving, hunting, and shipbuilding from Homer; of plowing and shepherding and how to make offerings to appease the gods. His battle scenes show a startling knowledge of human anatomy, and though they occur again and again—often in the same words—the episodes throw us right into the crunch of combat.

Greek tradition says that the Trojan War took place in the 12th century B.C., and archaeological and linguistic evidence supports the claim. The Greeks—Homer refers to them at different times as Argives or Achaians or Danaans—were an alliance of small kingdoms, each with its own rulers, powerful clans, and legends. In the Trojan War, a federation of these Greek kingdoms mounted a great political expedition across the Aegean Sea. They sailed to Troy, on the west coast of Asia Minor, also known as Ilios (that's where the name *Iliad* comes from).

Why did these Greeks undertake such a complicated and faraway venture? If we are interested only in history, we might suggest that they wanted to capture the lucrative merchant trade monopolized by Troy, which was strategically located on the edge of the Black Sea, between Asia and the West. If we are intrigued by poetry—and the *Iliad*, for all its historical accuracies, is above all a work of poetry—we must take into account the legend of Helen of Troy and move into the world of myth that surrounds the Argive warriors.

Mythological Background

The *Iliad* focuses on one small part of the Trojan War, nine years into the siege. (Homer's audience would already have known the details of how the war started and how it ended. Each poem in the Epic Cycle dealt with a particular part of the story, and even if the other poems were written later than the *Iliad*, the whole story most likely was common knowledge.) There are really two wars narrated in the *Iliad*: one between the Greeks and Trojans, and one among the gods themselves. And two legends explain the beginnings of the Trojan War.

The first concerns Helen, the daughter of Tyndareus and Leda (though she is also said to have been sired by Zeus, who took the form of a swan to ravish Leda). Helen was the most beautiful woman in Achaea. When she was of marrying age, suitors flocked from all over Greece to offer her gifts and marriage. Her father Tyndareus was afraid to antagonize any of these powerful kings and princes by choosing one of them. Odysseus, the king of Ithaca, suggested that they all swear to support whoever among them was chosen. The lucky winner was the very rich Menelaos of Sparta, brother to King Agamemnon of Mykenai, which was the most powerful of the Greek kingdoms.

The second legend concerns Paris, one of the sons of King Priam of Troy. Handsome young Paris was placed in a predicament by Zeus. At the wedding of Peleus and the sea goddess Thetis, Eris (whose name means "strife") threw down a golden apple, with the inscription "for the fairest" written on it. Unwilling to decide whether the apple should go to Aphrodite, Athene, or Hera, his wife, Zeus turned the sticky question over to Paris, who happened to be wandering on Mount Ida near Troy. Each goddess tried to bribe Paris to choose her, but Aphrodite offered him the love of Spartan Helen which, backed up with the goddess's own undeniable beauty, swayed Paris to her cause. From that point, Hera and Athene vowed revenge on Paris' home town, Troy.

The two legends then came together.

Paris went to Sparta as a guest of Menelaos. While Menelaos was away on a mission, Helen ran off to Troy with her handsome guest, becoming Helen of Troy. The Greeks, having sworn to defend whoever married Helen, gathered together a massive naval force to sail for Troy. Some say raising the army took ten years. According to the figures in Book II of the *Iliad*, the force assembled had more than 1100 ships and between 50,000 and 100,000 men. The Achaians camped on the beachhead near the plain of Troy and besieged the city unsuccessfully for nine years, making occasional forays into neighboring towns, looting gold and carrying off women for their pleasure. This is where the *Iliad* begins—occupying a few weeks in the siege of Troy and centered around the great Argive warrior Achilleus and his battle with the Trojan prince, Hektor.

The *Iliad* never shows us the fall of Troy, though it foreshadows it. According to legend, the Greeks later persuaded the Trojans to accept an offering of a giant wooden horse. Once the horse was inside the gates, the Greeks jumped out from their hiding place within it, opened the gates of the city, and sacked Troy. Helen was taken back by Menelaos, and the Achaians sailed for home. Of course, another poem—the *Odyssey*—tells us about that journey home, focusing on Odysseus' voyage back to Ithaca.

THEMES

1. WAR AND PEACE

The *Iliad* takes place during a fierce war between the Trojans and Achaians. Almost the entire poem is devoted to the fighting, from an initial overview of the forces to minute descriptions of combat. The descriptions of battle wounds and death are shockingly accurate; reading them, we cannot help but feel the bitterness of war. Since the two major characters—Hektor and Achilleus—either die or have their death foreshadowed, a sense of futility is also built into Homer's chronicle. And yet, posed against the viciousness is a sense of heroism and glory that adds a glamor to the fighting. Homer both abhors war and glorifies it.

Against the conflicts taking place on the plain of Troy, the domestic scenes within the city walls have a sweetness and sorrow. Along with the similes that tell of peacetime efforts back home in Greece, these scenes serve as contrast to the war, reminding us of what human values are destroyed by fighting, as well as what is worth fighting for.

2. THE HEROIC CODE

The concept of heroism and the honor that results from it is one of the major currents running through the poem. Achilleus' struggle revolves around his belief in an honor system opposed to Agamemnon's royal privilege. In a way, his struggle is one of faith: can he continue to believe in the ideals for which he has fought so valiantly and relentlessly? If not, what values can he hold onto? His conflict is not just with Agamemnon. War itself threatens the very code it supports. We see fighter after fighter enter the fray in search of honor; fighter after fighter is slain before our eyes. These men are certainly heroes: they are strong and courageous and larger than life. But posed against the backdrop of war, is their struggle worth the sacrifice?

3. ANGER AND RESPONSIBILITY

In the original Greek, "anger" is the word that opens the *Iliad*—Achilleus' anger and the destruction it brought to the Achaians. One of the major themes of the poem is thus Achilleus' coming to terms with his anger. In a broader sense, we can read this as man's need to take responsibility for his actions and emotions. Viewed this way, the *Iliad* is a poem of psychological and emotional growth. Achilleus must learn to civilize his rage. The tragic stake for this lesson is the death of his closest friend, Patroklos. Similar to Achilleus' anger is Agamemnon's *ate*, the moral blindness that descends on him and causes him impulsively to mistreat Achilleus. He, too, must learn responsibility for his actions and apologize.

4. MORTALS AND IMMORTALS

The gods and goddesses on Olympos, all-powerful and often ridiculous, are contrasted to the mortals, so seriously engaged on earth. The immortals are gigantic; they live forever and have nothing to fear. Beside them, humanity seems small, yet at the same time it gains tragic stature. Though the mortals are puny in comparison, there is something ennobling about their struggle to find value and moral meaning in their lives, and something heroic in the wholehearted way they engage in their pursuit. These men, whose lives are so clearly bounded by time and the fates, play out their destiny with fervor and depth of feeling. It is the gods, in fact, who often seem casual and small-minded. The *Iliad* shows us a human world filled with struggle and brutality, a world nevertheless in which mortals exercise *will* in the face of divine intervention—to create their lives according to their own terms of value, to suffer existence and discover its possible meaning.

STYLE AND STRUCTURE

The *Iliad* is composed in a traditional epic measure known as dactylic hexameters. This means each line is made up of six metrical feet. The first five feet in the line can be either a dactyl (one long and two shorts, $-\smile\smile$) or a spondee (two longs, $--$); the last foot is always a spondee. Thus the poem has a formal rhythm that is consistent throughout and yet varied from line to line. This regularity made it easier to memorize, while the variety prevented it from being monotonous (imagine hearing the same beat over and over again for 15,000 lines!).

Though the version we have is divided into 24 books, this was probably the work of later editors of the poem, or perhaps the books marked natural breaks in the work where the reciting poets took a rest or the reciters were changed.

You will notice many phrases—sometimes whole passages—repeated verbatim throughout the *Iliad*. These formulaic sequences are probably part of a whole fund of stock phrases that the oral poets had at their disposal. It has been shown recently that many of these formulas are based on metrics; they occur mostly at the ends of lines so they can fulfill the demands of the meter. In the same way, many of the descriptive phrases that are linked with a certain character happen to match the number of syllables in a hero's name.

The epithets are one of the most famous stylistic elements of Homer's verse. Such phrases as "swift-footed Achilleus," "Diomedes of the great war cry," "Hektor of the shining helm," or "Agamemnon the lord of men" are repeated again and again. Sometimes they seem to become part of the characters' names themselves. They define the characters by putting them in their social roles—such as "the lord of men"— or by showing how their heroic stature is due to a particular skill or virtue. Even if the epithets were added simply to fill out the metrical line, each time we hear them we feel their force. The warriors grow to legendary dimension from having their qualities as well as their names repeated.

It has been estimated that one third of the *Iliad* is repeated phrases, and perhaps much more than that is part of a formulaic oral tradition. Yet Homer's use of these handed-down words becomes his own virtue. He has been compared to an artist working in mosaic: the brilliant blue, red, and gold glass pieces are his stock phrases; the final design and its execution are his alone.

The epithets show Homer working with his traditional material, but the extended similes bring vivid, firsthand experience into the poem. A simile compares one thing to another; in the *Iliad*, the comparisons take us out of the battle and into other areas of human experience, where events are equally tense and crucial.

Often, the similes depict scenes of domestic life, cultural and agricultural settings that take us back to daily life in Achaia. They inform us of the Homeric world in its larger context and make the poem almost a social encyclopedia.

Other similes are about animals. Creatures of the hunt, especially lions and boars, call to our attention savage, instinctive qualities, making the battlefield seem at times like a jungle. We realize how war tears at the thin fabric of human culture, exposing the beast beneath.

Sometimes the similes are about natural catastrophes, extremes of weather that topple fragile trees and flood the land. Just as natural destruction is evitable, so is the fate of the armies as they clash in battle. The longer these similes grow, the more details Homer works in.

Two other stylistic elements are worth noting here. Homer often introduces a character and then offers a capsule history either of his noble genealogy or of his heroic deeds. Sometimes the characters tell their own histories. Nestor, for example, will recite his accomplishments the first chance he gets. These stories may seem like digressions, but they generally heighten the social nature of the poem. They place these characters within the context of their homelands and their families. More than that, these telescopic stories must have given Homer's listeners a sense of their own past, of their ongoing social order and values. One of the functions of a poet in a traditional oral society was to give this historical dimension, to connect his listeners with their past and project a future for them. In a culture like theirs, where few people, if any, could read, history itself was passed on by word of mouth. In the *Iliad*, if the warriors feel that their deeds are worthy of history, they imagine themselves being sung of by the bards of future generations. In Book VI, Helen even goes so far as to suggest that Zeus had wrapped her and Paris in his web of destiny "so that hereafter/we shall be made into things of song for the men of the future."

It is also good to keep in mind that the *Iliad* is composed in large part of long speeches, either in dramatic monologues or informal dialogues. This format may have offered opportunities for dramatics during recital of the poems. It's certainly easier to follow a long poem like the *Iliad* when the voices do not just alternate back and forth, but take time to express their characters in depth. This also gives the poem an immediate presence. We hear of people doing things, but if they have something to say they say it to each other right before us. Similarly, there is almost no interior dialogue in the poem. These are characters who *speak*, rather than just *think*. Even Homer communicates with his muse in direct speech: "Sing, goddess," he implores in the first line of the *Iliad*, and the poet sings.

The Story

BOOK I

Homer opens the *Iliad* by calling on the goddess or muse for divine inspiration. Then he tells us the theme of his poem—the anger of Achilleus and the resulting troubles it brought to the Achaian warriors. He sets forth another important theme, too: "the will of Zeus."

NOTE: The Trojan War is not mentioned by name. Homer assumed that the readers (or listeners) would be familiar with the legend and characters. What's really important to Homer is the dramatic and psychological dimension to this legend. That's why he centers his poem on a human story—the tragedy of Achilleus.

Homer quickly fills us in on the details of an argument in the Achaian camp. During their siege of Troy, the Achaians have been raiding neighboring towns. In one such raid they take as prizes two women: Chryseis, the daughter of the priest Chryses, and the fair Briseis. As the poem begins, Chryses has come to the Achaian camp to ransom his daughter. Although the Argive army agrees to the ransom, Agamemnon, the commander-in-chief, who had taken her as his prize, refuses. Chryses then turns to a higher authority; he prays to his god, Apollo, who favors him by sending a plague on the Achaians, which rages for nine days.

On the tenth day Achilleus, the greatest warrior among the Achaians, calls a general assembly of the army and suggests they ask their soothsayer Kalchas why Apollo is angry with them and what can be done to appease him. The seer reluctantly tells them the truth: unless Agamemnon gives the girl back, the plague will continue.

Kalchas was right to be nervous; Agamemnon is outraged. He insists that the girl is his prize, and if he's forced to give her up he will demand someone else's. At this point Agamemnon is the one who appears hot-tempered and unreasonable; Achilleus is calm. He responds that all the prizes have already been distributed, but Agamemnon will be awarded riches from a later expedition. Achilleus and Agamemnon here begin to stake out their opposition, which will underlie the plot of the entire poem.

NOTE: Keep in mind that the Achaian army was made up of many kings and their followers, each with its own tribal pride. Prizes determined in part the honor of each group. As the quarrel develops, this sense of social honor and rank will support Agamemnon's position. Achilleus' reaction is more emotional: Why should he or another be forced to give up something he's rightfully won? Two definitions of honor clash, one based on rank, the other on a person's actual ability.

The quarrel increases. Agamemnon threatens to take Briseis, Achilleus' prize. Achilleus, furious at this provocative insult, reminds Agamemnon that he has been fighting—and fighting valiantly—for ten years, not only for his own sake but for Agamemnon and his brother Menelaos. Formerly, Achilleus was content to accept small gifts while Agamemnon always got the best. He has respected the social organization that far. But now Achilleus threatens to leave the war with his men and sail for home. You can imagine how the warriors would gasp at that threat.

Agamemnon is adamant: if he must return Chryseis he will take Briseis. Achilleus' anger mounts. He considers killing Agamemnon then and there, but as he begins to draw his sword, Athene comes and stays his hand. The old counselor Nestor also tries to calm the quarrel, but without success. After freeing Chryseis, Agamemnon claims Briseis, and Achilleus, in turn, vows to fight no more on behalf of the Argive cause.

Weeping in desolation, Achilleus calls to his mother, the sea goddess Thetis, and asks her to intercede with Zeus on his behalf so that the Trojans will be temporarily victorious, dramatic proof that the Achaians can't win without Achilleus. As the gods assemble on Olympos, Thetis pleads her case to Zeus who agrees reluctantly, for he knows that his wife Hera favors the Achaians.

NOTE: Two motifs announced at the beginning will work through the entire poem: "the anger of Peleus' son Achilleus" and "the will of Zeus." Achilleus leaves the poem in Book I, not to return until Book IX, and not actually to rejoin the battle until Book XVIII. Yet all the time his presence is hovering over the poem, since we know that at any moment his arrival could turn the tide of battle in favor of the Achaians. During this time Achilleus, the great man of action, is inactive, and this forces us to probe his mind instead of his deeds, to figure out *why* he is behaving the way he does. You will probably find that your feelings toward Achilleus change over the course of the poem. When the Argives are being slaughtered you may feel his holding back is self-indulgent in the worst way. On the other hand, you may also be aware of the enormity of his idealism, his willingness to sacrifice everything for what he believes to be right and just. His own feelings and their context are extremely complex; all his actions—sulking, raging, and fighting—are written large for the Achaians.

The will of Zeus is demonstrated in his *plan*, which becomes a kind of scaffolding on which the *Iliad* rests. As readers you are privy to the devices of this plan, while the Trojans and the Achaians are at its mercy. Zeus' plan is another way of describing the consequences of Achilleus' anger. To the Greeks, the world was acted out in harmony with the gods: whatever took place was part of a divine plan. In the *Iliad* only you and the immortals are clued in beforehand as to what will take place.

BOOK II

Zeus sends Agamemnon a false message in a dream, saying that now is the time to marshal the Argives for victory. Agamemnon calls the army into assembly but instead tells them it's time to return home; they are getting nowhere in the war. Perhaps he is testing their valor or assuming that the force of their honor will give them a greater enthusiasm to fight than if they were merely obeying his command. Much to his surprise, the men leap to their feet and run to their ships, eager to sail. Athene, alerted by Hera, appears to Odysseus and urges him to stop the soldiers from fleeing.

Obediently, Odysseus reassembles the forces. When they are gathered, Thersites, an ugly man of no rank, abuses Agamemnon. His speech is a kind of parody of Achilleus' former scolding. For the Greeks, physical beauty was a sign of moral beauty, so we might see in Thersites' misshapenness a lack of heroic character as well; after all, he's urging them to give up. Odysseus and Nestor, on the other hand, rouse the Achaians to stay and fight. Agamemnon agrees, and retires with the highest commanders to make offerings to Zeus. We, however, know this won't have any effect. "He spoke," Homer tells us, "but none of this would the son of Kronos accomplish,/ who accepted the victims, but piled up the unwished-for hardship."

Much of the rest of Book II urges us to feel the scope of this drama. The first long simile of the poem compares the assembling army to "swarms of clustering bees that issue forever/in fresh bursts from the hollow in the stone . . . fluttering in swarms together this way and that way." We are told the earth groaned under the weight of the multitude. Agamemnon reminds the army that there are ten Achians to every Trojan. Most important, a series of similes emphasizes the size of the Achaian army: their bronze shields light up the scene with the force of a forest fire; their numbers are compared to flocks of wild marsh birds; the sound of their horses' feet makes the plain of Skamandros thunder. And as they take their position in the fields, they are themselves compared to the innumerable wildflowers that appear in spring. Finally,

> Like the multitudinous nations of swarming insects
> who drive hither and thither about the stalls of the sheepfold

in the season of spring when the milk splashes
in the milk pails:
in such numbers the flowing-haired Achaians
stood up
through the plain against the Trojans, hearts
burning to break them.

The entire Achaian host is then marshaled for the so-called "Catalog of Ships." This section of almost 300 lines describes all the ships, commanders, and contingents assembled for the Trojan War.

NOTE: It isn't important to read and remember every name on this long list. Many of the figures described here have little part in the rest of the poem. Many scholars have even suggested that the Catalog of Ships wasn't written by Homer. It seems, nevertheless, to be a fairly accurate account of the geography and politics of Mykenaian Greece. Whether or not it was written by Homer, he places it here to great effect. Its sweeping power gives the poem a sense of epic dimensions. In reading it, you are actually forced to experience the grand scale of the poem. It's like a long, slow sweep of a movie camera over a huge crowd scene. The longer it goes on, the more actors it reveals, until we feel awed by such a monumental event.

After the Achaian army is inventoried, Zeus sends a messenger to the Trojans, and there follows a somewhat shorter catalog of the Trojan army and its allies. Though the battles in the rest of the poem are almost always described man to man, the size of the army has now been set up as a dramatic background. Many human lives will be involved in every turn of the armies' fortunes.

BOOK III

The Trojans and Achaians meet for combat. Menelaos and Paris (Alexandros) single each other out, but then Paris shrinks from the encounter. His brother Hektor chides him for his good looks and his running after women, and especially for refusing to fight the man he wronged. Paris explains that his beauty is the gift of Aphrodite, not of his own doing.

Paris suggests that he and Menelaos meet in single man-to-man combat. The victor will win Helen, and the lives of the warriors will be spared. Everyone agrees to the terms, and the Trojan king, Priam, is sent for to seal the pledge. This duel sets up the symbolic nature of the war: it's being fought over Helen, and for the sake of Menelaos and Paris. These two fighters also stand for the two armies that face each other throughout the poem.

Meanwhile Helen is in her chamber at Troy, weaving a robe on which is depicted the battle of the Trojans and Achaians. Note that she is embroidering a pattern of events that she herself has brought about. Later, in Book VI, she'll say that the war is being fought for the sake of the poem that will sing about it. We are kept conscious that the events here will echo through time.

Helen is summoned by Zeus' messenger Iris to appear on the Trojan fortification wall. While there, she describes to Priam the different commanders of the Argive army.

NOTE: This is one of the most famous passages in the *Iliad*, known as the "teichoscopia" ("view from the wall"). Some readers have suggested that this episode, as well as the single combat, would have been more likely to occur in the beginning of the war, not in its tenth year. But though Homer is not at the beginning of the war, he is at the beginning of his poem, and he must set up certain poetic structures. On the wall, Helen is a vision of beauty, and her divinelike presence will drift through the entire poem, as its cause and inspiration.

On the battlefield, Menelaos and Paris prepare to do battle. This is the first of many one-on-one fights that Homer uses to personalize his battle scenes. Paris carefully puts on his armor, one of several similar descriptions in the *Iliad*. It's as if, like an athlete warming up or an actor putting on his makeup, the soldier heightens his nerve for battle with each separate piece of equipment he puts on.

Paris throws his spear at Menelaos but misses. Menelaos hits Paris but doesn't wound him; as he moves in on the Trojan, Aphrodite snatches Paris away, spiriting him back to Troy. Aphrodite then appears to Helen and urges her to go to Paris. Helen argues with the goddess, suggesting that Aphrodite go herself if she thinks he's so beautiful. But in the end, under the goddess's threats, Helen goes to Paris and lies with him in bed. Why does Helen argue here? Perhaps she's acting out her own conflict: should she be with her lover, Paris, or her husband, Menelaos? When she gives in to the will of the goddess, it's as if she's giving in to her own desires for Paris. The two of them meet in love while the battle is set to clash about them; Homer shows us his understanding of the "blind" nature of love and sexual attraction, which set this whole tragic situation in motion.

Meanwhile, Menelaos is left raging on the battlefield, looking for his vanished opponent.

BOOK IV

Now we move to Mount Olympos, where the gods sit in council. Zeus suggests that since Menelaos seems to have won the battle (by default), perhaps it's time to stop the fighting. But Hera and Athene are intent on bringing further destruction to the Trojans, and at their urging Zeus gives the command to let the war continue. This scene has a mixture of frivolity and bloodthirstiness. The gods' councils are almost parodies of human ones—yet their power is so much greater, it seems foolish for them to be quibbling like mortals. Their morals sometimes even seem lower than those of the warrior heroes. Since gods and goddesses are already immortal, they aren't concerned with heroic action as mortals are. Homer shows us how capricious and indifferent the destiny that rules us can be. But it is also clear that Homer uses his deities simply for comic relief.

Athene convinces a Trojan, Pandaros, to break the truce by shooting an arrow at Menelaos. The arrow draws blood although it doesn't seriously wound Menelaos. Agamemnon is tenderly concerned about his brother. As a physician comes to attend Menelaos' wound, the Achaians and Trojans again prepare themselves for battle.

Agamemnon, as commander-in-chief of the forces, rouses his men to fight, passing among the ranks and stopping to encourage his greatest commanders. The scene shows Homer's understanding of psychology; each of these great warriors reveals his personality in the way that he replies. First Agamemnon speaks glowingly to Idomeneus, leader of the Kretans, then to the two Aiantes (Telemonian Aias and Aias, son of Oileus). Next he rouses the old commander Nestor, who, mentally vigorous in spite of his age, urges his troops and charioteers to hold their ranks in battle. Agamemnon then encounters Odysseus, whom he chides for not getting ready more quickly. Odysseus responds angrily, defending his past valor. Agamemnon is quick to apologize, laughing. Either he was playing with Odysseus, or he has already learned enough from his quarrel with Achilleus to keep his fighters' tempers in check. Agamemnon visits Diomedes and rebukes him too for holding back. In contrast to Odysseus, however, Diomedes accepts the king's words, respecting his rank and understanding his motivation: he's not rousing the men to anger; he's rousing them to fight.

The Trojans and Achaians meet in a furious battle, attended by the war god Ares and three allegorical figures: Terror, Fear, and Hate. (Put yourself in a soldier's boots. Aren't these the most likely emotions you'd feel?) The fighting is severe and many men are killed. Apollo urges on the Trojans, reminding them that the Argives are without their greatest warrior, Achilleus, who ''beside the ships mulls his heartsore anger.'' Athene, for her part, prods the Achaians, guiding their hands to destruction.

NOTE: The battles in the *Iliad* are methodical and progress logically from step to step, keeping our interest with very sharp detail. As the poem goes on, you'll notice that opponents in battle seek not merely to kill each other but to dishonor each other's corpses by removing their armor. Homer uses this to further the fighting: a warrior who steps forward to remove his victim's armor becomes a likely target for another's spear. But the act is a matter of honor, not to be taken lightly; a warrior's armor is an important sign of his dignity. Both will be of immense importance later in the battle between Achilleus and Hektor.

BOOK V

The furious battle continues. On the Achaian side Diomedes distinguishes himself most of all. This book has been known since ancient times as the *Diomedeia*, because it is here that Diomedes achieves his *aristeia*, his highest moment of glory in the war. He is fighting so fiercely and thoroughly that Homer tells us we might not be able to tell which side he is on. When he's shot by Pandaros' arrow, he has it pulled out without flinching.

The gods are now flinging themselves into the battle. Athene comes to Diomedes and promises to guide and protect him. Note that the goddess visits Diomedes when he is exhibiting true heroic grit: we could see this as not a physical visit, but another way of describing his heroism and prowess. Athene tells him not to fight the gods if he recognizes them—except Aphrodite.

Diomedes rages against the Trojans, killing many and wounding Aineias, Aphrodite's son. When she comes to carry her son off the battlefield, Diomedes strikes her with his spear, piercing her skin so that the *ichor*, which immortals have instead of blood, flows from it. This is a shocking moment and must have been especially so for Homer's audience. Aphrodite's beautiful form should be above the ravages of war, and Diomedes might be going too far. The goddess departs in pain to Olympos, where she's comforted by her mother Dione, but Zeus simply warns her to keep away from war.

Ares, the bloodthirsty god of war—sometimes he's referred to as war itself—now enters the battle on the side of the Trojans, inspiring Hektor to rally his forces. The Danaans fight bravely, but they're steadily pushed back by Hektor and his Ares-inspired men.

Hera and Athene—who hate Trojans, remember— are furious with Ares for interfering, and they plead with Zeus to let them interfere on behalf of the Achaians. He agrees, and Athene dresses herself for battle, arming herself with the terrifying shield called the *aegis*, hung with the figures of Terror, Hatred, Battle Strength, Onslaught, and the grim Gorgon.

NOTE: The *aegis*, belonging to Zeus but frequently wielded by Athene, is the ultimate offensive and defensive weapon. Homer, whose descriptions are usually so specific, seems almost to back away from anything so powerful. The *aegis* is essentially a goatskin shield, but its name in Greek also suggests "stormcloud" or "hurricane wind." When it is shaken in the face of the enemy, the effect is one of total terror. In the middle of the shield sits the *literal* head of Medusa, the snake-haired creature whose face had the ability to turn men to stone. Perseus killed Medusa, cut off its head, and gave it to Athene to use on the *aegis*. The *aegis* will be used later in the *Iliad* by both Apollo and Achilleus, and in the end it will cover the corpse of Hektor.

Thus armed, Athene together with Hera rouses the courage of the Argives. Athene appears to Diomedes, who has been keeping back from the fray, both because of his wound but also because Athene had earlier warned him not to fight any god but Aphrodite—and Ares was clearly present in the murderous Trojan attack. Athene not only lifts her ban but also pushes aside Diomedes' charioteer and rides with him into battle herself. They meet Ares, and Diomedes spears him in the belly. Howling "with a sound as great as nine thousand men make, or ten thousand,/ when they cry as they carry into the fighting the fury of the war god," Ares flees to Olympos. Thus Diomedes wounds a second god during his *aristeia*. Again, Zeus shows little sympathy; he simply finds Ares' bloodthirstiness offensive.

Diomedes' success seems stunning. He has killed many Trojans and wounded two gods. We wonder: Will the Argives have to pay for his boldness? Athene and Hera return to Olympos, leaving the mortals to fight it out for themselves—for the time being.

BOOK VI

Diomedes continues his *aristeia*, and the Achaians fight strongly. Menelaos captures Adrestos alive, and he's just about to spare his life for ransom when Agamemnon hotly urges him to kill Adrestos and all the rest of the Trojans, even "the young man child that the mother carries/still in her body." Agamemnon stabs the captive. This scene seems particularly cold-blooded. Maybe Homer is offering us a contrasting character study in the different attitudes of the two brother-kings. Or he may be contrasting two views of war; perhaps Agamemnon is right—since they are at war they should ruthlessly kill all the Trojans, and then we may feel differently about the casualties of war. Homer is certainly shading his story, but there is no easy answer to the problem of what is moral in a time of war.

Meanwhile, Glaukos and Diomedes face each other for combat; but when they discover their ancestors had been friends, they put down their spears and exchange armor in a gesture of friendship. This is in stunning opposition to the scene with Menelaos and Agamemnon, and shows a nobler side to the Achaians. It also lets us ease into the gentle, domestic scenes within the walls of Troy.

At the same time, this scene sets a note of sorrow, of mortal loss, that pervades Book VI. Glaukos' lines to Diomedes are some of the most beautiful and saddest in the poem. "Why ask of my generation?" he says;

> As is the generation of leaves, so is that of
>   humanity.
> The wind scatters the leaves on the ground, but
>   the live timber
> burgeons with leaves again in the season of
>   spring returning.
> So one generation of men will grow while
>   another dies.

There is simple wisdom in the statement, but also the sense that it's vain for mortals to strive after immortality. This is a key to the heroic concept, where it's important to die well.

Hektor arrives at the city, planning to make offerings to Athene to calm her rage against the Trojans. First he meets his mother, Queen Hekabe, and urges her to gather the women to offer prayer to Athene. Then Hektor goes to Paris' house and criticizes him for hanging back from the fighting. Helen adds her own, surprisingly not very flattering description of Paris and bemoans her fate that will be sung by the poets to come. Paris and Helen seem antagonistic here, after their lovemaking. In dramatic contrast, we next see the loving relationship between Hektor and his wife Andromache.

Hektor goes to find his wife, who has been watching the battle in distress from the city towers. Andromache, crying, runs to greet her husband and pours out her heart to him, begging him to stay home. Throughout this scene Homer's descriptions are extremely emotional, and the feeling he shows between husband and wife (and child) seems absolutely modern, especially compared to the formal, heroic tone of the rest of the poem. Based on these passages, many modern readers have decided they felt more sympathy for the Trojans than for the Achaians, and they assume that Homer had similar feelings. But any compassion we may feel for the Trojans should heighten our sense of the tragedy of Achilleus, as well. Homer's intimate portrait of life in Troy highlights the terrible conflict between war and peace. Even though Hektor would rather stay with Andromache, he offers instead what is practically a credo for the heroic age:

> All these
> things are in my mind also, lady; yet I would
>   feel deep shame
> before the Trojans, and the Trojan women with
>   trailing garments,
> if like a coward I were to shrink aside from the
>   fighting;
> and the spirit will not let me, since I have
>   learned to be valiant
> and to fight always among the foremost ranks
>   of the Trojans,
> winning for my own self great glory, and for my
>   father.

Hektor reaches out to hold his son, but the boy is at first frightened by his father's helmet. Hektor then leaves to join Paris.

Up until now we've understood what Menelaos and his Argives are fighting for; now we know what Hektor is fighting for—Troy, his home. Yet we know Troy is doomed: Hektor himself tells us "there will come a day when sacred Ilion shall perish." The book is full of tragic foreshadowing. Hektor carefully describes how he has imagined his wife being taken captive after the fall of Troy; it is a heartrending account. Andromache has already told us she is an orphan, and now she tells Hektor that "you are father to me, and my honoured mother,/you are my brother, and you it is who are my young husband." Yet we know that Hektor too is doomed to die, and we ache for Andromache's loss. Andromache departs from Hektor, "turning to look back on the way, letting the live tears fall."

BOOK VII

Hektor and Paris return to battle. Athene and Apollo meet and decide it's time for a break in the fighting. Under their guidance Hektor's brother Helenos proposes that Hektor challenge the Argives to man-to-man combat. Athene and Apollo watch the scene disguised as vultures—rather disturbing forms for gods to take.

Hektor issues his challenge, and though the Achaians at first cower at the suggestion, they eventually draw lots and Aias is chosen. Hektor and Telemonian Aias battle, with Aias getting the upper hand. Before anything conclusive happens, the heralds break up the fight on the grounds that night is coming. Hektor and Aias exchange gifts in a display of formal tribal etiquette. Interestingly, anthropologists have discovered that certain peoples today still follow similar customs.

Nestor, the wise old strategist, proposes that the Achaians take time out to burn their dead, and then build a ditch and fortifications to protect their ships. Meanwhile at Troy, Antenor rises and suggests that the Trojans return Helen and all her possessions to the Argives. Paris refuses to give Helen back, but he does agree to return her possessions. Priam urges Idaios to go to the Achaians with Paris' offer and adds the suggestion that a truce be made so that the dead may be gathered and burned. Both sides need to take a rest from war.

The Achaians resist any ransom but agree to the temporary truce. The Trojans gather their dead. In a solemn scene they wash the corpses and lift them onto wagons. They're bursting with sorrow, yet Priam commands them to stay silent. The Achaians also gather and burn their dead, and then build fortifications around a ditch. These battlements will figure heavily in the fighting to come.

On Olympos, Poseidon (who with Apollo had built the giant walls of Troy) says he's annoyed with the Achaians for not making a sacrifice before building their walls, but really he is afraid their Mykenaian workmanship will outlast his. Zeus promises Poseidon that after the Achaians return home he can swallow their walls in his waves. (Some commentators have suggested that in this scene Homer was offering a reason why these marvelous Achaian walls were no longer standing.) Zeus thunders disagreeably all night long. The solemn image of the two burning funeral pyres remains.

BOOK VIII

This book really belongs to Zeus. We feel his ability to be present everywhere, watching every little action. At no other point in the *Iliad* does he influence the action so directly. The Greeks understood that thunder and lightning were the language of Zeus, the means by which he spoke directly to mortals; watch how he uses them, to warn mortals and to threaten the other gods.

Dawn rises. At an assembly of immortals Zeus warns the gods and goddesses not to interfere in the Trojan War. In a muscle-flexing speech, he warns them that in a tug of war against all of them he would still be the victor.

The battle continues at Troy. Zeus, having come down to Mount Ida, raises his golden scales, placing in each end the fates of the Trojans and the Achaians. The Achaian fate lowers as the Trojan fate rises, so we know beforehand that the Trojans will triumph today. Zeus shoots a flash of lightning over the terrified Greeks. Many readers have wondered whether Zeus controls fate or is controlled by it: the answer isn't entirely clear from this passage. Zeus has already announced to us the plan of his will, so in a sense the scales are merely demonstrating poetically what he has already decided. On the other hand, the scales of fate may really be the means by which Zeus reaches his decisions. Zeus uses the scales again in Book XXII to decide the fates of Hektor and Achilleus.

Now Nestor and Diomedes charge at the Trojans. Zeus lets loose a bolt of lightning that lands in front of their chariot, scaring the horses. Nestor, recognizing Zeus' work, advises Diomedes to turn back. Diomedes is loath to flee from his heroic duty (remember, after yesterday he has quite a reputation to keep). He's afraid that Hektor will taunt him as a coward—and, indeed, Hektor does just that. Diomedes ponders whether to turn his horses around and fight Hektor. Three times he starts to turn, and each time Zeus thunders a warning not to. Diomedes and Nestor finally leave, and Hektor boasts to the Trojans that the tide is turning in their favor. Here the intervention of the gods seems more solemn and definite than the free-for-all of the day before.

Hera inspires Agamemnon to rouse the Argives, and their spirits revive. Teukros, brother to Telemonian Aias, kills several Trojans with his bow and arrow, darting out and then running back to find cover beneath his brother's shield. But Hektor stops Teukros with a stone that breaks his collarbone. Again the Trojans push the Achaians back toward their ditch.

Hera and Athene can't bear to sit back and do nothing; they prepare to go down to aid the Achaians. Watching all, Zeus sends them a warning via his messenger Iris: if they interfere, he will lame their horses and give Athene and Hera lightning wounds that won't heal for ten years. The goddesses think better of their plans.

Zeus returns to Olympos to speak to the sulking Hera and Athene, explaining his intentions:

> For Hektor the huge will not sooner be stayed
>   from his fighting
> until there stirs by the ships the swift-footed son
>   of Peleus
> on that day when they shall fight by the sterns
>   of the beached ships
> in the narrow place of necessity over fallen
>   Patroklos.

Thus Zeus clearly announces his plan, which is actually the plot of the poem. We are reminded that the events taking place are leading up to the return of Achilleus. From here on the immortals generally interfere less in the doings of the war; Zeus' plan simply works itself out, inexorably.

Hektor assembles his forces for the night, and they camp on the plains of Troy, their fifty thousand campfires burning like the stars in heaven. Again, imagine this as a vast panorama in a movie, the night sky reflecting the army camps.

BOOK IX

Agamemnon once again summons the Achaians together. He notes that victory seems to be with the Trojans and suggests they turn their ships toward home. Diomedes, still high on his recent success, furiously rebukes him and vows to stay. The other Achaians shout their agreement. These are the same men who fled to their ships in Book II; they seem nobler now. Again, Nestor adds the voice of wisdom, saying that Diomedes' argument is incomplete. It's time, he says, for a feast, and then Agamemnon should follow the advice of his best counselors.

At the council of the lords of the Achaians, Nestor speaks the rest of his mind. He urges Agamemnon to apologize to Achilleus so they can get him back fighting for their side.

Maybe Agamemnon's had time to cool down; maybe he realizes that the battle's getting serious and he has to put his people's interest before his pride; or maybe it's just easier to give in during a privy council than in front of his army. At any rate, Agamemnon now admits he's been blind and rash. He reels off the numerous treasures he will offer to Achilleus—gold, horses, the girl Briseis, land, even his own daughters, and more. He can't resist adding at the end, however, that Achilleus should yield to him because he is "kinglier" and the elder. Odysseus, Telemonian Aias, and Phoinix (an old family friend of Achilleus) are sent as ambassadors to Achilleus.

NOTE: At his hut Achilleus is singing with a lyre a poem about heroes. This poem within a poem is a special self-conscious touch by Homer. (In the *Odyssey* a poet sings to Odysseus a poem about the Trojan War.) No one but Achilleus sings poetry in the *Iliad*; it's like the highest honor Homer, a poet himself, could give to a character.

Most of the rest of this book is six long speeches, in which the ambassadors try to persuade Achilleus to accept Agamemnon's apology, and he refuses.

Homer shows his knowledge of the classical art of rhetoric—polished formal argument—but more than that, he subtly reveals these characters' personalities in the way they talk and what they say. Odysseus explains the situation to Achilleus. He recounts the gifts Agamemnon is offering (cleverly leaving out the last part of Agamemnon's speech). Achilleus answers Odysseus brilliantly, and his argument is worth studying; it's the deepest insight we get into his thinking. He uses a complex series of rhetorical strategies, and readers have had many differing opinions about them.

Why, asks Achilleus, should anyone fight, so long as the weak and the strong are honored alike? In other words, if a warrior's gifts of honor (such as Briseis was) may be taken away at a whim, he's left with no honor gained. Achilleus claims he feels especially dishonored since he was the only one whose prize was taken away.

Also, he cleverly points out, isn't the war being fought for the sake of a woman—Helen—who was taken from one man by another? His case is pretty similar; why shouldn't he be allowed to be as outraged as Menelaos was? Agamemnon can keep his gifts, Achilleus says. They're worthless without honor. He tells Odysseus that Thetis had told him he had two fates: either to win glory at Troy and die young, or to go home safely but live unknown and unhonored. What would be the point of dying for glory, if it can be so easily taken away? Thus Achilleus reveals that he's not just hurt beneath his anger; he also feels the heroic code is being questioned. We can see how profoundly he's shaken by that.

Some readers have felt, however, that Achilleus' arguments here are the beginning of his downfall. Agamemnon has admitted his fault and offered a generous recompense, yet Achilleus holds onto his anger. This seems mean-spirited, and it seriously imperils the lives of his fellow fighters.

Phoinix tries to convince Achilleus to return to battle by telling him the story of Meleagros who, in a similar situation, waited too long and regretted it. This is clearly the speech of an old man; like Nestor's speeches, it's full of digressions and parables, and he adds a tug on the heartstrings, reminding Achilleus that he practically reared him.

NOTE: Included in Phoinix's argument is the allegory of the prayers. This describes the relationship between prayers, or asking forgiveness, and the ruin, or blindness, that follows one who does not have the sense of courage (or humility) to admit wrong. These figures are startlingly personified by Homer, and their purpose is right to the point of the argument. Agamemnon has already admitted to his blindness; shouldn't Achilleus be next? The root word for blindness is *ate*, conceived as something that takes over a person, clouding his judgment. Along with anger, it is one of the major moral themes of the *Iliad*.

Aias also tries to convince Achilleus, but he won't be moved. The messengers return glumly to Agamemnon. Diomedes recognizes that Achilleus will fight only when he's ready in his heart. They all retire for the night.

BOOK X

In contrast to the formal, noble councils of Book IX, we plunge now into an episode of night, confusion, secrecy. Some scholars believe this book was at one point a story on its own and was only later worked into the *Iliad*, either by later editors or by Homer himself. It is, in any event, a gripping interlude. It isn't easy to get a moral handle on it: it has a ruthlessness that may be meant to counteract the heroics of war.

Neither Agamemnon nor Menelaos can sleep, they're both so distraught with the way the battle's going. They decide to send a spy to the Trojan camp to discover the enemy plans. Diomedes volunteers and chooses Odysseus as his companion. Under cover of night, the two stealthily make their way toward the Trojans, guided by the cries of a heron sent by Athene.

Hektor and his commanders can't sleep either. Hektor too sees the need for espionage; he offers a reward to the scout who will steal toward the Achaian ships. A man named Dolon rises to the bait. This book is, in fact, often called the *Doloneia*, after this unfortunate Trojan scout. He's a kind of Trojan counterpart to Thersites in Book II. Dolon is described as evil-looking, exhibiting greed rather than intelligence. He wears a wolf pelt and martin's cap, which may leave you with a weasily impression of him.

Dolon is sighted by Diomedes and Odysseus before he can get very far, and he's clearly no match for them. Homer describes the two Achaians as "rip-fanged hounds" after some wild prey, and Dolon is literally trapped by them. You may even feel that Diomedes and Odysseus toy with Dolon as a cat toys with a mouse before it gobbles it up. Such behavior doesn't reflect much glory on the Achaians—or on the Trojans, if Dolon is their representative. Dolon gibbers with his teeth chattering. Odysseus tells him not to fear or worry about being killed, but his smooth talk is just a way to get information from Dolon on the setup of the Trojan camp. Dolon tells all, particularly mentioning the recently arrived contingent of Thracians, led by King Rhesos, who has in his possession some extraordinary white horses. Having gotten all the information they need, Diomedes abruptly beheads Dolon; his "head still speaking dropped in the dust."

NOTE: Some readers have seen these actions of Odysseus and Diomedes as barbarous and deceitful. Others defend them legalistically, saying that although Odysseus promises Dolon no fear of death, Diomedes is the one who kills him.

Notice that the Achaians never get a chance to use any of this information. This episode does nothing to further the plot. It does, however, show a seamier side of war. The Greek audience, too, probably enjoyed Dolon's stupidity, and Diomedes and Odysseus' easy victory over him.

Odysseus and Diomedes surprise the Thracians while they are sleeping. Diomedes kills thirteen men, including the king, and Odysseus drags their bodies out of the way to clear a path for the horses. Again, the action is so calculated it makes you feel these two heroes are very bloodthirsty. The Achaians escape with Rhesos' fabulous horses and return to camp. Diomedes and Odysseus cleanse themselves in the sea, as if to wash away the gore.

BOOK XI

At sunrise the allegorical figure of Hate mounts the ship of Odysseus and gives a terrible cry to rouse the Achaians.

Agamemnon elaborately dons his armor. The arming of Agamemnon is very carefully detailed: his rich armor with its heraldic symbols emphasizes the power of his rank rather than his personal qualities. Athene and Hera cap off his arming with a crash of thunder, "doing honour to the lord of deep-golden Mykenai." Later we'll see Achilleus' divinely crafted armor, especially in Book XVIII. The elaborately wrought panorama of Greek life shown on his shield will give Achilleus human and moral stature, as well as supernatural strength, in contrast to Agamemnon's kingly status. This is the longest of Homer's ritualistic arming scenes. It prepares us for the coming *aristeia*, this time Agamemnon's. With enormous power, Agamemnon kills Trojan after Trojan. He's compared to a lion—as befits his royal station—and to an obliterating fire that "comes down on the timbered forest/and the roll of the wind carries it everywhere, and bushes/leaning under the force of the fire's rush tumble uprooted." Under Agamemnon's leadership the Achaians push the Trojans back toward their city wall, as far as the Skaian Gates. But it's only a temporary triumph; Zeus gives word to Hektor that after Agamemnon is wounded victory will be with him. Agamemnon is soon stabbed through the elbow with a spear and is forced to leave the battlefield.

One by one the great Argive heroes are wounded. It's as if Homer is creating a vacuum, which will cry for someone (Achilleus we hope) to fill it. Diomedes is pierced through the foot by an arrow from Paris (Alexandros). Homer, who's always careful to add characterization to his war scenes, shows Paris laughing at his own work (archers never look as dignified in Homer's poems as spear-throwers or sword-fighters do). Diomedes, not at all frightened, scoffs at Paris, and with characteristic unflinching bravado, has Odysseus pull out the arrow.

Odysseus' short speech to himself is interesting. This is the closest Homer comes to actually presenting a character's thoughts in the *Iliad*; Odysseus is literally thinking out loud. Odysseus feels the pressure of the heroic code of honor: "[I]f one is to win honour in battle, he must by all means/stand his ground strongly, whether he be struck or strike down another."

But Odysseus is wounded next. Telemonian Aias steps forward to cover the flanks as the Argives retreat. When Machaon, a physician, is hit, Nestor drives him in his chariot back to the encampment. Hektor spurs the Trojans on. Eurypylos is the fifth Achaian commander to be wounded.

Achilleus has been watching the rout while perched on the stern of his ship. We can tell from this that Achilleus is by no means unconcerned for the Achaians. He is double-minded, wanting to fight for glory and yet wanting to hang back for honor. He asks his best friend Patroklos to find out if the man he sees being led from battle is Machaon—though perhaps he is also hoping Patroklos will find out more about the battle in general. This is the beginning of Patroklos' involvement, acting as a surrogate for Achilleus. It's also the beginning of his downfall.

Patroklos meets Nestor, the garrulous old man, who regales him with some long anecdotes. Nestor has an ulterior motive: he wants Patroklos to urge Achilleus to join the fight or, if that fails, to put on Achilleus' armor himself to fool the Trojans. Nestor is one of the most elaborately conceived characters in the *Iliad*, and his long-winded speeches are consistently of the same order. They bring in history—often Nestor's own—and legend to serve as moral examples to whomever he is addressing. Nestor tends to wander, and he loves to dwell on a past glory that he can no longer achieve in battle, but he is clearly the elder statesman of the *Iliad*, and his councils are often the deciding factors that turn the plot.

Patroklos is persuaded by Nestor's speech. Before returning to Achilleus he stops to help the wounded Eurypylos.

BOOK XII

The Trojans move closer to the defensive wall of the Achaians. Notice how clearly Homer makes us see the battlefield layout; we're always conscious of that wall. We know from the opening lines that it's doomed to fall, but we're on the edge of our seats waiting for it to happen. At first the wall seems enormous—so large, we've been told, that it stood through the rest of the war and took the combined might of Apollo and Poseidon to bring it down. Its strength comes to stand for the strength of the entire Argive army. But as Hektor and his forces approach, the focus on the wall narrows.

Poulydamas suggests to Hektor that the Trojans dismount from their chariots and move on foot through the ditch, which is stuck with pointed stakes. Some readers have noted that Poulydamas is a foil for Hektor, showing by contrast his superior qualities. Poulydamas is Hektor's counterpart to Achilleus' comrade, Patroklos, but they aren't so loyal to each other. Though Hektor here agrees with the advice of Poulydamas, they seem to have been enemies somewhere in the past.

The Trojans arrange themselves in five companies to attack the wall from different directions. We skip around to various parts of the wall where the fighting is continuously furious. As Poulydamas, Hektor, and their men debate by the edge of the ditch, a sign from Zeus appears. A high-flying eagle clutches in its talons a blood-red snake that writhes backward and bites the eagle. The snake falls amid the battle as the eagle flies away, screaming in pain. This is serious. Omens were part of religion in those days; this isn't just a bad luck charm, like a black cat, but a definite warning of the gods' displeasure.

Poulydamas suggests to Hektor that the omen portends a turn of events for the Trojans even though things now appear to be going well. Hektor indignantly scoffs at the reading: "[O]ne bird sign is best," he said, "to fight in defense of our country." Thus Poulydamas' prudent counsel is contrasted to Hektor's impetuous and heroic nature.

The Trojans press against the fortifications from one side and another. The two Aiantes seem to be everywhere, fending off the attack for the Argives. Finally Hektor picks up a gigantic stone, hurls it at the main battlement gates, and crashes through them. Hektor's breach of the gates is achieved in a cinemalike montage: first the gate, then the stone, then the doors of the gate, the double door-bars, the holding pin, back to the stone, the gates groaning, door-bars breaking into splinters, and the face of Hektor following the stone through the broken doors. It's one of the most careful and artistic delineations of battle in the *Iliad*, and it is a decisive turning point for the Argive forces.

In through the wall pour the raging Trojans, eager to burn the Achaian ships. Hektor's dark face is like night, but his eyes gleam fire. The Achaians flee in terror among the ships. The *Iliad* has reached its halfway point.

BOOK XIII

While Zeus is preoccupied, Poseidon harnesses his underwater chariot and drives across the sea to help the Achaians. He appears to the Achaians in various disguises and inspires them. The book descends into a long and vicious battle, giving the second rank of Argive heroes a chance to shine.

The fighting in Book XIII is the most ruthless in the poem and is descibed by Homer in particularly bloody detail. There can be no doubt that we are in the midst of a terrible war, and constantly the hideous details of battle counteract the heroic struggle. Eyeballs pop out of a severed head, a head is thrown at the enemy like a bowling ball, and taunts are made over dead warriors in a way unlike other battle scenes. The combatants are vicious and merciless. But Homer's goals are always poetic. The vividness of the fighting makes war *real*, and just as the relentless mortality critiques the heroic code, it also brings it to life poignantly— and in deadly seriousness.

Hektor moves against his enemies like a great stone (remember he broke through the fortification wall also with a stone). The fighting all around is thick. Idomeneus, leader of the Kretans, is aiding a wounded comrade behind the battle lines. He runs into Meriones, his nephew, who is plucking out another spear, and the two engage in a long duel of taunts. Notice that much of the inspiration to fight in the *Iliad* comes from fear of shame; even the gods rouse the warriors by shaming them. Idomeneus defines courage and cowardice by talking about an ambush: while a coward would turn colors and chatter his teeth, a brave man would stand his ground, ready and eager for combat. Idomeneus and Meriones take an inventory of the battle positions around the wall and decide to enter on the left, where the Argive defense is weakest.

Idomeneus fights famously—this is his *aristeia*. We have another of Homer's graphic descriptions of death, as Idomeneus slays Alkathous:

He cried out then, a great cry, broken, the spear
  in him,
and fell, thunderously, and the spear in his
  heart was stuck fast
but the heart was panting still and beating to
  shake the butt end
of the spear.

The image of a spear throbbing with the last pulsations of a dying heart epitomizes the beauty and horror of war. Aineias leads the Trojans against Idomeneus until Idomeneus' age forces him to retire. The gruesome fighting continues. Menelaos fights several Trojans.

In the center of the fray Hektor continues his ravaging, while the two Aiantes defend the wall like yoked oxen. Poulydamas once again counsels Hektor, telling him to draw back temporarily and with his commanders devise a plan of attack. Hektor agrees with the plan of action but, battle hungry, he suggests that Poulydamas himself call the assembly while he, Hektor, fights on.

NOTE: As with most of the great fighters in the *Iliad*, Hektor's fighting frenzy borders on madness. In their *aristeias*, these warriors rise to a lunatic state of prowess. But this eagerness to fight is also at the root of the conflict that we will later see hurling a hero to his fated end.

Hektor ranges the ranks looking for several of his commanders, but all of them are dead. He does find Paris and once again rebukes him. Paris defends his fighting, and together the two enter the battle where it's thickest. They lead the Trojan advance like a tidal wave.

As Telemonian Aias defends the Argive position, an eagle appears, a good omen for the Achaians. Hektor again misreads the sign, claiming it predicts a Trojan victory. The hideous sound of battle rises to Olympos.

BOOK XIV

Behind the lines the Achaian ships, so numerous they can't all sit in the water, have been drawn up onto the beach. There, Nestor, Odysseus, Agamemnon, and Diomedes gaze woefully at the ruined Argive defenses. For the third time Agamemnon suggests it might be time to head for home. Odysseus and Diomedes insist it's time to fight—even though they are wounded—and they reenter the battle. Agamemnon's continued desire to flee certainly makes us question his ability as commander-in-chief.

Poseidon gives a battle cry to rouse the Achaians (much the same yell as Ares gave when he was wounded in Book V). Hera, watching from Olympos, is happy with Poseidon's work but wants to make sure that Zeus, who's still distracted off on Mount Ida, doesn't notice that they're interfering again. Hera devises a plan to distract Zeus further. The ensuing passages, known to the ancient commentators as "The Deception of Zeus," offer some comic relief in the middle of this most hideous battle. Hera prepares to seduce Zeus by bathing, perfuming, and dressing herself up. It's almost a parody of the way we've seen the warriors arm for battle. She enlists the aid of Aphrodite to make her irresistible. Hera also calls on the allegorical figure of Sleep, brother of Death, to help her by visiting Zeus with his mind-dulling power.

Hera makes her way to Mount Ida. Before she's even finished with her flattery and lying, Zeus, struck by her sexy beauty, calls her to bed. Hera suggests going to her underwater chamber where they'll be safe from prying eyes (and also, she knows, safe from Zeus' eyes seeing anything at Troy), but Zeus can't wait. He catches her in his arms and lays her down. The earth spontaneously blossoms into a cushion of "fresh/grass, and into dewy clover, crocus, and hyacinth" beneath them. The whole scene provides not just comic relief (like most of the scenes on Olympos in the *Iliad*), but also a sweet and sympathetic reminder of the pleasures that go on far removed from the grim reality of war. This makes the war seem more tragic, especially when we remember that sweet love scenes like this between Paris and Helen started the war in the first place.

After the lovemaking, Zeus falls asleep, and once more Poseidon goads on the Argives. The fighting's as fierce and gruesome as in the previous book; wounds are portrayed in gut-wrenching detail. Telemonian Aias stops Hektor with a large rock, hitting him in the chest and bringing him to his knees. The Trojans quickly take Hektor away from the battle as he spits blood. The Argives, growing bolder during Hektor's absence, fight savagely, holding off the Trojan advance. Aias, son of Oileus, fights particularly well, chasing the retreating Trojan troops.

BOOK XV

The Trojans are finally pushed back across the ditch. Zeus awakens and immediately discovers what's been happening. He scolds Hera, threatening to punish her; she offers a flimsy excuse that stops just short of lying. He commands her back to Olympos to summon Iris, his messenger, and Apollo to him. Then, in the most explicit terms yet, he explains to Hera the outline of his plan—that is, of course, the plot of the poem. Notice that Homer's drama doesn't depend on surprises: he pushes his characters toward a destiny we can easily foresee. It's the relentless approach of fate that provides the dramatic tension, as the characters draw closer to their tragic ends.

Hera does not tarry or meander. Homer tells us she goes fast as "the thought flashes in the mind of a man who, traversing/much territory, thinks of things in the mind's awareness,/'I wish I were in this place, or this', and imagines many things." This extraordinary image shows Homer's understanding of how the mind works—how complex our desires are, and how swiftly the brain functions. Hera arrives at Olympos and maliciously tries to goad Ares into interfering with the battle by telling him of the death of his son, Askalaphos. Only Athene's prudent hand stops Ares from getting involved.

Iris and Apollo go to Zeus, who's intent on manipulating the war again. Apollo wakens Hektor from his wound-stupor and breathes new strength into him. The Trojans attack once more, led by Ares brandishing the *aegis*. He stares straight into the eyes of the Danaans, shakes the terrible *aegis*, and raises a battle cry that terrifies them into a stampede. Like a child playing with sandcastles, Apollo kicks down the Achaian wall and bridges the ditch for the Trojans. They rush for the ships.

Patroklos, still tending the wounded Eurypylos, sees the rout taking place. He hastens to Achilleus to ask him to intervene.

The battle continues, with Hektor and Aias in the thick of things. Teukros aims his bow at Hektor, but Zeus causes the arrow to miss its target. It is now clear that the gods have abandoned the Achaians and are on the side of the Trojans.

Hektor urges his men to attack. This is the great assault of the Trojans, and Hektor is justly in his glory. Yet he is, like Ares, "insatiate of war," and while the beautiful horse goes to his sweet river and pasture, Hektor goes into battle, where the river is bloody. Following this simile comes another in which he is compared to a great lion that puts some hunting dogs to flight.

Another powerful series of similes attends Hektor's battle frenzy as he breaches the defense of the ships. First the Achaian defense is compared to a "towering sea cliff" that holds back the shifting winds and huge waves. Then Hektor is compared to a "storm-fed wave" that batters a ship and shakes its sails with a hurricane force. Finally Hektor is compared again to a lion that attacks a flock of oxen, and though the shepherd can tend to the first and the last he cannot keep the lion from devouring an ox in the middle and causing the rest to stampede. These wild and naturalistic forces add an almost mystic fury to the battle scenes, and they appropriately build up Hektor at the moment when he is most dangerous to the Achaians.

BOOK XVI

Patrokolos, weeping at the Achaian defeat, comes to the hut of Achilleus and recounts the extent of their losses. He accuses Achilleus of being inhuman and asks to wear his armor so that the Trojans will think Achilleus has reentered the fighting and will lose heart.

This is the fatal turning of the plot for both Achilleus and Patroklos. Patroklos will take Achilleus' place and will, in fact, die for him. Achilleus' tragedy will take shape: he will move from shame over loss of honor to grief and guilt over the death of Patroklos. Achilleus repeats his reason for holding out against Agamemnon—he refuses to accept that rank (Agamemnon's) could eclipse honor (Achilleus'). Ask yourself—do you think Achilleus has held out so long that his anger makes him look petty? The price he'll soon have to pay—his friend's life—is extreme, and Achilleus himself will wonder if it was worth it. As he is hurled toward his fate, notice how Achilleus' public anger turns into a private sorrow, making him seem deeper, more human, and more of a tragic figure.

NOTE: Though he is sticking to his position, we can clearly see that Achilleus is being moved closer to a decision to fight. He's no longer standing aloof; he's watching the battle and is seriously concerned. That is why he goes along with Patroklos' scheme.

Achilleus is beginning to plot military strategy, too: he tells Patroklos to push the Trojans back from the ships but not to rout them all the way back to Troy. He offers two reasons: 1) so that he may still win honor when he reenters the battle and 2) because Apollo or another god may be aiding the Trojans and will break him if he pushes too far.

Meanwhile, Telemonian Aias is still valiantly defending the ships from the Trojans, but he's growing tired. Hektor shatters his spear, and the Trojans bring fire to the Achaian ships. Achilleus sees it happening and hastens Patroklos toward the fatal battle. Patroklos slowly and ritualistically arrays himself in the armor of Achilleus—all but the great spear, which only Achilleus can lift. Achilleus rouses his followers, the Myrmidons, from their fifty ships, fetches his sacred goblet, and makes a prayer to Zeus to grant

Patroklos victory in battle and to send him safely back to him. Homer notes forebodingly that Zeus "granted him one prayer, and denied him the other.

Just as was planned, the Trojans tremble at the sight of Patroklos, thinking Achilleus has returned. Many are caught in the spiked ditch and slaughtered; others are penned in between the ditch and the beached ships. In the fierce combat Sarpedon, the son of Zeus, faces off against Patroklos. Seeing what's happening, Zeus starts to save his beloved son but Hera talks him out of it. She warns that if he interferes, other gods will want to do the same on behalf of their favorites. Death, after all, is the inevitable lot of all humans. That is summed up in the very words used to describe the two classes of beings: mortals (those who die) and immortals (those without death). Zeus relents.

Sarpedon is slain. Glaukos, magically healed of his wounds by Apollo, brings news of Sarpedon's death to Hektor, which reinspires him to fight. Apollo retrieves Sarpedon's body from the battlefield and brings it home for a proper burial.

Patroklos is on a rampage now and pushes the Trojans back to the wall; he's forgotten the warnings of Achilleus. He tries to take the wall but Apollo warns him back.

Finally Hektor heads directly for Patroklos, and the two battle over the body of Kebriones. The two sides rage into the afternoon. Three times Patroklos rushes the Trojans. On the fourth try, Apollo hits him in the back, then literally unarms him, striking off his helmet, spear, shield, and corselet. This process is the reverse of the ritualistic arming scenes, and you may feel that a new ritual is being proposed: preparation for death. The process is terrifying, and Patroklos himself is frightened. Stupefied, he is speared in the back by Euphorbos, and there's little left for Hektor to do but finish him off. In his dying speech, Patroklos points out to Hektor that the Trojan prince had little to do with his death. "No," Patroklos says, "deadly destiny . . . has killed me."

NOTE: We've seen many warriors killed in this poem, but Patroklos' death seems supremely unfair. That, of course, may be all to Homer's purpose. Do you find yourself sympathizing with Patroklos? Do you think Hektor's boasting is at best empty and at worst murderous? If so, you are probably feeling what Achilleus will feel and will be able to identify with his indignation and rage.

BOOK XVII

Menelaos stands astride the fallen body of Patroklos like a cow lowing beside its calf. A battle begins, both for Patroklos' armor and for his body.

The heavy fighting shows how deep a dishonor it was for a corpse to be stripped, and how great a prize it was for an enemy to carry off the armor. Patroklos, of course, was wearing the armor of Achilleus, which would have been especially valuable. The dishonor may be seen as reflecting on Achilleus as well.

The struggle finally centers around the body of Patroklos—as it will later around Hektor's—and how it is about more than honor. It was believed that a corpse must have proper burial rites in order for the soul of the dead person to pass through the underworld. In Book XXIII, in fact, we will see the shade of Patroklos appear to Achilleus and beg him for proper rites so he may pass through the gates of Hades. Forbidding this ritual would be like dealing a double death to an enemy.

The encounter between Menelaos and Euphorbos shows how powerfully Homer can bring emotion to a single character in the midst of a mélée. In a few lines Euphorbos is brought before us and taken away, but because of Homer's detailed descriptions and simile, his death is extremely touching. He shows compassion in his retort to Menelaos—concern not just for his fallen comrade but for his grieving widow and parents back home. And when Euphorbos' lovely braided hair (Homer is careful to show us its "locks caught waspwise in gold and silver") is bloodied in his fall, Homer compares him to a

> slip of an olive tree strong-growing that a man raises
> in a lonely place, and drenched it with generous water, so that
> it blossoms into beauty, and the blasts of winds from all quarters
> tremble it, and it bursts into pale blossoming. But then
> a wind suddenly in a great tempest descending upon it
> wrenches it out of its stand and lays it at length on the ground; such
> was Euphorbos of the strong ash spear . . .

Though Euphorbos had a hand in the killing of Patroklos, his youth and beauty are mourned in passing by the poet.

The fighting is furious, and Menelaos wonders if he should stay and fight. His soliloquy is much like Odysseus' in Book XI. This time, however, the warrior decides it is prudent to flee. Hektor, therefore, gets Patroklos' armor and proceeds to arm himself. Both sides clash over the body, and the tide turns again and again. Hektor and Aineias lead the attack for the Trojans; Menelaos and the great Aias put up a noble Achaian defense. The two sides have a tug-of-war over the corpse, like tanners stretching an ox hide. The divine horses of Achilleus weep over the death of their friend and will not be moved until they are inspired by Zeus.

The battle rises to a high pitch, emotional and unclear. Athene comes to rouse Menelaos in his warfare; Apollo comes to Hektor. The tide of victory shifts continually as Zeus rattles his *aegis*. Menelaos tells the news of the death of Patroklos to Nestor's son, Antilochos, and bids him bring the terrible news to Achilleus. The Achaians gain the corpse and Menelaos and Mariones carry it away from the battle. But the Trojans press against the weary Achaians like a roaring forest fire.

BOOK XVIII

Antilochos comes to the hut of the worried Achilleus and delivers his message: "Patroklos has fallen, and now they are fighting over his body/which is naked. Hektor of the shining helm has taken his armour." This is his terrible moment of truth and Achilleus' response is instantaneous. He smears dust over his head and face, falls to the ground, tears at his hair, and cries hideously.

Realistically, at this emotional crisis there is no eloquent speech Achilleus can make. We must trace for ourselves what brought him to this point. This is the ironic fulfillment of his own wishes that the Achaians might be brought low before him; this is the result of his anger that began the poem. At his supposed moment of glory, he is hurled to the ground in agony. What started out as a stand for honor has become the torture of guilt and terrible responsibility. His honor is in the dust. Thetis hears his tortured cry; as she returns from the sea we remember the first time she undertook this journey, to set the plan in motion for Achilleus' revenge. Now the revenge has cruelly completed itself.

Achilleus bemoans the loss of Patroklos and curses the day he fed his anger. Yet Achilleus knows he must live by the code he has chosen. If he has nourished himself on anger so far, he will not turn to honey now. Instead, he will turn his wrath from Agamemnon to Hektor and avenge the death of Patroklos.

We must be careful not to lay an easy judgment on Achilleus, for this isn't an easy road to take. To reclaim his honor, he chooses death—he pursues Hektor even though Thetis tells him this will ultimately mean his own death. The tragedy of Achilleus is that he must play out the events he himself set in motion. Everything he does, he does on a heroic scale. Just as he grieves to the fullest, so shall his revenge on Hektor be fought to the height of heroic glory.

Thetis goes to fetch new armor for Achilleus and urges him not to fight until she has brought it back from Hephaistos. But the Achaians are still struggling over the body of Patroklos, and Hera notices that Hektor is about to drag it back to Troy. Hera sends Iris to tell Achilleus to appear as he is before the Trojans. With the help of Athene, Achilleus makes his first appearance on the battlefield—unarmed! No one else, of all the heroes we've seen in the *Iliad*, matches this superhuman presence. Suddenly the full character of Achilleus reveals itself. The *aegis* thunders about his shoulders; a cloud cracked with flame circles around his head. Is he one man or a whole army? Follow the similes: he is likened first to an entire encampment blazing with fires, then to the trumpet-cry of attackers besieging a city. With the stormy *aegis* above him, his head flashing lightning, and bellowing a thunderous war cry, he resembles no one so much as mighty Zeus. It's no wonder the Trojans are stricken with terror. Such an entrance heightens by contradiction our feelings toward Achilleus. Perhaps, a moment ago, you were ready to lay the finger of blame on him; now he is simply awesome.

Poulydamas wisely counsels Hektor to return with the army to the safe walls of Troy, but once again Hektor refuses his friend's advice. Now that Achilleus is on the scene, Hektor's resistance to caution simply looks foolhardy. He is hurtling toward his own fate, with *ate* (delusion) attending him, hastening him along. Meanwhile, Achilleus and the Argives mourn the death of Patroklos, cleansing his body and wrapping it in sheets.

Thetis reaches the home of Hephaistos and tells him of Achilleus' predicament. In his smithy, with twenty bellows blowing the fires, Hephaistos creates new armor for Achilleus, particularly an extraordinary shield inlaid with gold and silver. The description of the shield of Achilleus is probably the most famous section in the *Iliad*. In this one extended image, Homer depicts his ideal social order and cosmic order, and places them both within a work of art. Scholars disagree as to whether the shield shows life during Homer's period or during the Mykenaian period; probably it has parts of both. But there is no doubting the shield's symbolic value and its importance to the poem.

The scenes drawn on the shield are so intricate, so full of life, it's hard to imagine how any single picture could show it all. Of course, the shield *is* an object of wonder: it was made by a god. The earth, sky, and sea are on the shield, and the constellations of the stars. Also on it are two cities. In one are festivities and celebrations, and though there's a dispute, it's handled within the context of the Law. But beside it is another city, besieged by war, attended by Ares and Athene in full battle gear. Here are ambush and massacre, women and children within a walled city, confusion and destruction in battle. Perhaps this reminds you of the city of Troy. And yet the other happy city is recalled in numerous similes throughout the poem, of farming and shepherding, of marriages and rich city life.

The shield is further elaborated with scenes of agricultural life and with a fabulous dancing celebration where young men and women perform elaborate maneuvers. Around these all runs the Ocean River, or primal Okeanos, the limits of the cosmos. Suddenly we are able to place the world of war within the context of total human existence. Some readers have felt the city at war on the shield seems out of kilter, implicitly criticizing the battle world of the *Iliad*. But others point out that two cities exist within the shield, and both must be seen together. Perhaps when Achilleus takes this shield into battle he is not simply fighting a battle, but protecting the values of an entire civilization and universe. What higher stakes could a poet propose for the actions of his characters?

The shield, even within the story, is proposed as a marvelous work of art. Perhaps you remember Helen's saying that the war of Troy is being fought for the sake of a poem. The shield of Achilleus is also a work of art within a work of art (the *Iliad*). What seems to be the divine craftwork of Hephaistos is actually the writing genius of Homer!

BOOK XIX

As dawn rises, Thetis returns with the divine armor for Achilleus, who is still mourning Patroklos. Before putting on his armor, Achilleus calls an assembly of the Achaians. He and Agamemnon begin to heal the wounds caused by their feud. Achilleus expresses grief over the outcome of events and questions whether the results were worth it. He resolves to put away his anger. Notice that Achilleus wraps up things quickly—he is impatient to begin the real fight. Remember, we have seen that he has already transferred his anger to Hektor in revenge for the killing of Patroklos. The feud with Agamemnon is old hat to Achilleus; his tragedy is taking him further than that.

Agamemnon also apologizes and admits that he was under the power of *ate*, or delusion. You can see from their respective speeches the different characters of Achilleus and Agamemnon. The king admits he made a mistake but blames it on a kind of outside influence that takes over someone. He proposes to give the gifts he offered before to Achilleus, worrying over technical details of his "contract" with Achilleus. Achilleus' response is entirely emotional: first grief and bitterness over the death of his comrade, then a desire to head right into battle, with no thought for the gifts, which, to him, are insignificant. To be fair, Achilleus never seemed to be holding out for more gifts; his was a stand for honor, not for gold. The physical, mortal world is not entirely his home (his mother was a goddess). He even suggests that the Achaians not eat, but just go ahead and fight.

Odysseus, showing his usual good judgment, explains that men must eat and will fight better because of it. He urges too that the gifts be delivered to Achilleus now, so that the affair can be properly wrapped up. After all, he says, the standoff between Achilleus and Agamemnon was not merely a personal quarrel. It involved all of the Argives, and it's fitting that they should all witness the healing exchange of gifts. Achilleus had been insulted in front of them—shamed by their eyes—and so he must be justified in the same social way. The exchange is made.

The girl Briseis is also returned to Achilleus. First she encounters the corpse of Patroklos and mourns his death. Homer once again brings a character to life in a flash. This woman who was previously a thing, a war prize, is suddenly revealed as a tragic figure, a terrible victim of war, an orphan many times (much like Andromache). Achilleus, too, mourns aloud for Patroklos, grieving his death more than if it were his father or even his son. Achilleus' lamentations are extreme; they border on madness, like his anger and his warrior rage. The closer we get to him, the larger he appears. Now the divine part of him becomes clearer, and you will see in the next book that it will take immortal power to counteract his seemingly immortal might. With his supernatural armor he readies himself for war. Mysteriously, one of his horses speaks to him, prophesying his death. "I myself know well it is destined for me to die here," Achilleus responds, "far from my beloved father and mother. But for all that/I will not stop till the Trojans have had enough of my fighting." This man who communicates with animals is more than human, and when he's in his fury he'll wage more than a human fight.

BOOK XX

On Olympos, Zeus calls the gods together. Afraid that Achilleus will overpower the Trojans before the appointed time, he urges them now to join the battle on whichever side they choose. It's as though Achilleus' entrance raises the fighting to a new level so that the gods must participate; we're building up to a great combat of mighty forces and terrifying intensity. And though the battle of the gods does not really get underway until Book XXI, Homer gives us an advance picture of the forces ready. Hades himself, god of the underworld, is afraid the entire earth will crack open, "and the houses of the dead lie open to men and immortals,/ghastly and mouldering." Such is the tumult raised by the combating gods.

We may also see in this fury a foreshadowing of the battle to come between the avenging Achilleus and Hektor, but we have to wait awhile for it. Achilleus slowly works his way to his *aristeia*, killing numerous Trojan warriors along the way. Aineias meets Achilleus face to face, the two hurling insults back and forth. But Aineias is fated to outlive the Trojan war and take over from Priam the royal legacy.

The fight between Achilleus and Aineias gives an interesting example of the way the passage of time is presented by Homer. His method is not strictly chronological. It can't be, because the swiftness of the gods' actions moves in supernatural, not mortal, time. (Remember the speed of a thought?) A whole conversation between Poseidon, Hera, and Athene takes place in the instant when Aineias raises a stone and Achilleus draws his sword. Again it may be helpful to think of movies. We are used to seeing in films simultaneous events placed in sequence, as in "meanwhile back at the ranch." This is Homer's method and, just as in movies, there is no intrusion of a narrator telling us what's taking place. The scene cuts back and forth as action is held in suspension. Before the fight really gets going, Poseidon snatches the Trojan from combat and places him down at the outer edge of the battlefield. His time for glory will come later.

Now it is Achilleus' time, and he continues his slaughter. When he kills Polydoros, Hektor's brother, Hektor moves in to face Achilleus. But once again a god interferes, delaying the climactic moment, as Apollo hides Hektor in mists Achilleus can't penetrate. So the great Argive warrior fights on, corpses in his wake, his revenge unfulfilled. Over fallen bodies and armor Achilleus makes his way, the wheels of his chariot splattered with blood and his hands covered with gore.

BOOK XXI

Achilleus drives the Trojans back across the plain toward Troy. Half of them fall into the river Xanthos (also called Skamandros) and in his war-frenzy Achilleus dives in, slaughtering in a circle around him. He chooses twelve live Trojans to take as captives; really they are live sacrifices to avenge the death of Patroklos. Shrink as you may, this should remind you that the *Iliad* portrays the values of its own age, not modern ones. Its society is still tribal, and its rites and rituals do not always fit within our concept of civilization.

But even Achilleus seems to have reached a turning point in his rage. When the Trojan prince Lykaon reaches out to him to spare his life, Achilleus won't listen, although he had spared Lykaon in a previous encounter. Achilleus is a changed man—changed by his wrath and changed by his destiny. As he moves through his tragedy the niceties of civilization drop away. In a famous speech Achilleus explains to Lykaon that his request for mercy is futile. Before the death of Patroklos such a thing might have been possible, but now no one can escape him. All are fated to die, even Achilleus, but sorrow over mortality cannot stand in the way of a heroic destiny. Lykaon is killed, sent to Hades. His poignant plea only emphasizes the warrior stature of Achilleus. In his rage Achilleus furiously taunts the corpse.

He fights on, killing many, stuffing the river with corpses. Finally the river god can stand it no longer and asks Achilleus to stop; his waters are being ruined. Achilleus agrees, but when the rivergod then calls out to Apollo to intervene on the Trojans' behalf, Achilleus dives into the water as if to slay the river god himself. In a fury the water rises, and a dramatic fight between Xanthos and Achilleus ensues. There is no other passage like it in the *Iliad*. Suddenly all the underlying forces of passion, rage, anger, and betrayal seem to be unleashed and become active partners in the conflict. As Achilleus struggles through flood and tidal wave you may feel he needed a god for a worthy opponent—mortals are not up to his level. Look at Achilleus now—caught in the furious current, battered by waves of corpses, losing his grip—and you can see the external manifestation of his internal conflict. Order has gone from his world, he is under sway of crazed passion, his "natural" world confounded. It takes the intervention of Hera and Hephaistos, who bring fire to the plain and make the river boil until it gives in, to calm things down. Really we might say Achilleus stands for his world, for the heroic values of archaic Greece, and in the midst of the Trojan War that world is being turned upside down. It is moving from myth and legend to tragedy.

After Hera and Hephaistos finish, all the gods join in the battle, fighting each other with an almost comic frenzy. Athene fights and wounds Ares and Aphrodite, Apollo and Poseidon taunt each other, and Hera smashes Artemis. Through it all Zeus remains impassive.

NOTE: This fight is known as the *theomachia*, literally the "battle of the gods." Some readers suggest it should be more serious, coming at this point in the story. A battle could hardly be more powerful, however, than the one we've just seen between Xanthos and Achilleus; perhaps we need a break at this point. Too, the idea of a mortal fighting a god is much more frightening than immortals fighting each other. They, after all, can't be killed, and so there is something naturally mocking in their actions. The *theomachia*, in fact, seems to *mimic* the horror of war, rather than heighten it. The gods are always amused at the foibles of mortals. Nevertheless, the gods fighting each other may show another example of the way war rips apart a culture's values.

At the gates of Troy, Achilleus meets the Trojan Agenor, who is being inspired by Apollo. While his attention is temporarily averted, the retreating Trojans stream through the open gates, gaining safety— for a moment.

BOOK XXII

Achilleus realizes he has been tricked by Apollo and returns to the battle. Priam sees him coming from the walls and sadly laments the fate that he fears awaits Hektor, his most princely son. This is the first of several speeches in this book that give us the human reaction to the events of the war. Priam may be a great king, but his grief makes us pity him. The order of his life has been turned inside out. He fears a horrifying and undignified end: that his own dogs will devour his body. Those who should be his domestic comfort will destroy him. Hekabe, Hektor's mother, also laments in anguish, both of them trying to convince Hektor not to fight Achilleus.

NOTE: In an action that is startling to our modern eyes, Hekabe pulls out her breast as if to show it to Hektor. Instead of having her say, "I am your mother,

I love you," instead of telling us anything *about* their relationship, Homer presents the object in the simplest and purest terms: Hekabe nursed Hektor at her breast, and that says all that needs be said about the depth of their relationship.

This is a striking example of Homer's art of direct presentation. He doesn't talk about things; he shows them to us. Characters don't think; they speak. He uses similes, not metaphors. In other words, things are not presented figuratively; they are compared, one explicit thing to another explicit thing. The *Iliad* is a world of particulars—that is one of the challenges of reading it. You must draw the conclusions yourself.

There are four speeches in the *Iliad* that read like a character thinking to himself; we've read Odysseus' and Menelaos' already. Now Hektor ponders whether to fight or seek safety in Troy. But he must follow his heroic principles, defending his family and citizens, even though it seems that from the beginning the war and its cause were distasteful to him. He resolves to stand and fight—until he sees Achilleus bearing down upon him. As Achilleus blazes toward him, Hektor turns and runs. From what we have seen of Achilleus, that's probably an appropriate response. Hektor's running away doesn't make him look like a coward as much as it shows us how awesome Achilleus appears. After all, we have just seen Hektor come to the difficult but heroic decision to fight. Now, however, he's out of his mind with fear, no longer capable of logical thought. Just as Achilleus is out of control in his wrath, he sends others out of control from fright. Hektor's running makes Achilleus loom larger.

Around the city they run, Hektor escaping and Achilleus pursuing. They're like olympic runners racing for a prize, Homer tells us, except they aren't running for a trophy: "No, they ran for the life of Hektor." Yet, as at a mere race, there are spectators. Watching from Olympos, Zeus wonders whether he should save Hektor. Athene reminds him that Hektor's destiny is already written, and Zeus sends Athene on her way to speed things up.

Achilleus continues chasing Hektor, who can't find a place to hide and can't get help from his allies behind the walls. Homer tells us they run as though in a dream. The inevitable weight of fate has compressed their lives into this one suspended moment. But it can't last for long. Zeus raises his scales, and Hektor's fate pulls him down.

Appearing as Deiphobos, Hektor's brother, Athene tricks Hektor into stopping to fight Achilleus. Hektor faces his opponent and suggests they first swear not to defile each other's corpses. Hektor, as usual, has something civil about him. He is fighting for home and country, fighting in front of his people, and he wants to uphold the social virtues. But Achilleus is far from home, far from domesticity, far into the depth of his passions, his war mania, and his revenge for Patroklos. No, he will swear no oaths. Achilleus spears Hektor through the throat. With his dying breath Hektor again asks that his body be returned to Troy for proper rites, but Achilleus refuses. The other Achaians come forward, and all stab the fallen Hektor. Achilleus strips the body of its armor and brutally pierces holes in Hektor's ankles, stringing hide through the holes and dragging the corpse behind his chariot, its head dragging in the dirt.

Many readers—especially modern ones—have felt such sympathy for Hektor in this passage that they have taken him to be the hero of the poem. Certainly Homer means us to feel the pathos of Hektor's death, but don't you also feel pity for Achilleus? Pity and awe, perhaps. For he, too, is filled with grief—for the death of his dearest friend. His fighting Hektor is based on that revenge. If he is ruthless, he is ruthless in grief now, not merely anger. And yet his anger *is* terrible. We see the absolute depth of it.

At the same time, Achilleus' uncontrollable rage perfectly expresses the deadly spirit of war. As our sympathy is roused for Hektor, it's also roused for the city of Troy and all that it stands for—civilization, home, and family. The tragedy of Achilleus is also the tragedy of Troy.

So in the most dramatic and touching terms, Priam, Hekabe, and Andromache mourn the death of Hektor. Andromache faints at the news, then laments out loud. Hektor's death, they know, is the end of the line for Troy. Andromache speaks of her son, Astyanax, who should be in line to rule the city. Instead, he'll be an orphan with a grim future; Priam's Troy is finished.

BOOK XXIII

Achilleus and the Myrmidons drive their chariots solemnly around the pyre of Patroklos and begin the funeral feast. In a dream, the ghost of Patroklos asks Achilleus to bury him quickly so that he may pass fully into the realm of the dead. In a touching plea, reminding Achilleus of their eternal bond of friendship, Patroklos asks that his bones or ashes be mingled with those of Achilleus in one gold vessel. A huge funeral mound is built and many sacrificial offerings are piled on it, including the bodies of twelve Trojan warriors. Patroklos is placed in the middle, and the pyre is lit, Achilleus mourning and lamenting all night long. In the morning Achilleus calls for funeral games.

NOTE: The scene reminds us that the world of the *Iliad* is one of ritual, from its repeated formula phrases through its stylized battle sequences and its code of honor and shame. This elaborate funeral and the rites of competition in the games show how valued Patroklos was, but they also show the importance attached to retrieving and burying the corpses of the warriors (as well as their armor, which may have been symbolic of the body itself). Though sometimes the gods in Homer seem frivolous, nevertheless mortals always give them their proper worship and respect. All must be done in specific order. The great funeral of Patroklos and the funeral games show us a formal world in which life is played out almost like theater. And we can assume that, as usual, the gods are watching.

A number of contests are waged: a chariot race, a boxing match, a wrestling match, a foot race, a fight with armor, a discus throw, an archery match, a spear throw. During these contests we are able, for the last time, to meet all the great Argive heroes: Odysseus, Diomedes, Aias, Menelaos, Idomeneus, Nestor, and Agamemnon. Though the proceedings are light and full of action, they may be seen as serving a function similar to a wake—easing the burden of death. We get to see Achilleus in a social role as leader of the Argives, and he thus appears human to us after the frenzy of his wrath. Throughout the games, Homer continues his vivid characterizations of the Achaian heroes: Odysseus the crafty; Nestor the long-winded, full of memories of youth. After the furious and bloody fighting of the preceding books, the formal contests and combats here return a sense of order to the poem, a hope for civilization after war.

At the last contest, the spear throw, Achilleus defers tactfully to Agamemnon. He gives the king first prize, not for winning the contest, but because they all know how much greater than the rest Agamemnon is with the spear. In a way, Achilleus is paying respect to Agamemnon's rank, not his ability, and this gesture—so opposite to the one that began all of the madness—begins Achilleus' healing journey out of anger.

BOOK XXIV

After the games are finished, Achilleus still doesn't stop mourning the death of Patroklos. Tossing and turning, he seems at times to be mourning the past, the entire series of events that make up the plot of the *Iliad*. Perhaps this final bout of grief prepared Achilleus for his final reconciliation. But not yet: in a pathetic gesture, Achilleus continues to drag the corpse of Hektor around the tomb of Patroklos, as if that might bring back the dead friend or further hurt the dead enemy. The gods, however, preserve the body of Hektor from decay or injury.

Zeus, once more looking from Olympos, sees there's no point for either side in Achilleus' actions. They do Achilleus no moral good and simply make the Trojans sadder. He calls Thetis to him and has her tell Achilleus that now is the time for Priam to ransom the body of his son Hektor. For once the interference of the gods is soothing. Our final view of them, like the final view of the Argives, shows things moving toward a more peaceful and natural order.

At Troy, in the midst of weeping and sorrow, Priam is told of Zeus' decision. He prepares to make his dangerous way to the Achaian camp. Hekabe pleads for him not to put himself into the hands of the man who has killed so many of his children, but Priam is firm. Firm, but not without fear. His irritation as he orders his relatives out of his house shows how nervous he is—another glimpse of the subtle ways in which Homer understands human psychology.

The god Hermes, called Argeiphontes, is sent to guide Priam across the plain of Skamandros to the Achaian camp on the beachfront. (Remember the difficulties Dolon had navigating this territory, and he would not have been nearly so great a capture for the Achaians as Priam.) Hermes leads the Trojan king past guards and watchpoints and lands him safely in the tent of Achilleus. Priam clasps Achilleus by the knees, and Homer seems to stop the action for a moment to let us feel the intensity of this extraordinary encounter. All we have seen throughout the poem is the hideous gulf of anger and war horror that can consume these two people—actually two *peoples*, for Achilleus and Priam now stand for the Achaians and the Trojans. We can feel as well the challenge implicit in the scene; it is dangerous to both men. Can Achilleus truly overcome his rage and move toward peace? Homer, always the master of his scene, knows that Achilleus and Priam feel these questions and tensions, too. Priam, "caught the knees of Achilleus in his arms, and kissed the hands/that were dangerous and manslaughtering and had killed so many/of his sons." And Achilleus "wondered as he looked on Priam, a godlike/man."

Priam urges Achilleus to think of his own father and then pity Priam in his outrageous position, a king "who must put my lips to the hands of the man who has killed my children." The moment is not lost on Achilleus. Both the Trojan king and Argive warrior weep for their sons, fathers, and comrades. This sharing of common grief becomes a bridge back to human sympathy. In an extraordinary speech Achilleus soothes Priam's sorrow by painting a picture of their common misfortune and the inevitable limits of mortality. These, says Achilleus, cannot be changed by grieving. Though the human lot he portrays is grim, his actions show a human decency that somehow softens our sense of what it means to be human. Grieving as one, they reinforce their common humanity.

Priam asks not to be seated so he can more quickly attend to the return of Hektor. Suddenly Achilleus' anger flashes out—he could kill the man in a minute! Homer is no sentimentalist. The complexities of Achilleus' character don't disappear instantly. But Achilleus puts away his anger, the word of intemperate wrath that began the *Iliad*. A strange healing power surfaces. There is no pretty ending; Troy, we know, will soon be destroyed. Yet by reaching out to Priam, Achilleus, for a moment, brings these two bitterly warring nations into a zone of peace. The scene is uncompromisingly tragic: Patroklos is dead, Hektor is dead, Priam will soon be killed, Achilleus will soon be killed. Yet somehow, in the midst of suffering, moral beauty survives.

Priam returns to Troy with the body of Hektor. The three great women of Troy lament him. Andromache mourns on behalf of their son and, for herself, mourns the loss of love's intimate comforts; Hekabe mourns for Hektor's heroic purity; and Helen (the last and the first) mourns and yet celebrates his kindness and generosity. Again, grieving becomes a testimony of human virtue. The Trojans build a great funeral pyre, and the rites for the burial of Hektor are completed.

NOTE: Observe how the plot structure of the *Iliad* completes itself. In the first book, a father (Chryses) comes to Agamemnon to plead for the return of his child but is refused. In the last book, a father (Priam) also pleads to Achilleus for the return of a child; this time pity is shown. Though this symmetry is surely there, Homer is an artist who permits complexities and contradictions. As you begin to sum up your feelings about the *Iliad*, test all the threads. The question is not simply is Achilleus right or wrong, or are the Trojans or Argives the real heroes. Homer values both cultures. He sees meaning in the heroic code but he also sees its shortcomings. In that same way, he pictures the horrible sufferings of a world at war and yet shows us the human dignity that can shine through. In the beginning Apollo says that mortals maneuver through Destiny with "the heart of endurance." That is where the *Iliad* begins and ends.

A STEP BEYOND

Tests and Answers

TESTS

Test 1

1. The *Iliad* starts with _____
   A. a description of the Trojan horse
   B. an invocation to the muse of poetry
   C. the quarrel between Agamemnon and Menelaos

2. Agamemnon's camp suffered a plague because of _____
   A. Achilleus' jealousy
   B. Apollo's anger
   C. Poseidon's interference

3. Homer opens his poem _____
   A. with a detailed background of the Trojan War
   B. with Thetis' visit to Zeus on Mount Olympos
   C. in the ninth year of the Trojan War

4. One thing apparent about Homer's gods was that _____
   A. they were all equally powerful
   B. they possessed exaggerated human characteristics
   C. they were always treated seriously in poetry

5. In Book II the army's desertion was halted _____
through the efforts of
    I. Athene
    II. Zeus
    III. Odysseus
  A. I and II only
  B. I and III only
  C. II and III only

6. The Book II survey of the Achaian host is _____
generally referred to as
  A. "The Shield of the Brave"
  B. "The High and the Mighty"
  C. "The Catalog of Ships"

7. Achilleus' flaw was _____
  A. in his heels
  B. his passionate pride
  C. his inability to think strategically

8. Paris agreed to a duel with Menelaos after _____
  A. he saw Helen's face
  B. a lecture from Hektor
  C. Aphrodite's intervention

9. Homer's technique with the beautiful Helen _____
was to
  A. describe her face in loving detail
  B. refrain from detailed description
  C. convert its one blemish into an asset

10. The destruction of Troy could be traced to _____
  A. the ill will of Hera, queen of the gods
  B. Agamemnon's breaking of the truce
  C. Pandaros' failed attempt on Agamemnon's
     life

11. What is the cause of Achilleus' wrath? Describe the
event and the reasoning behind his reactions. (See Book
I and Book IX.)

12. What are Homeric epithets? Describe their use. (See the Introduction.)

13. Who is the real hero of the *Iliad?*

Test 2

1. Book V, which describes the furious battles, has been called _____
   A. the *Aeneid*
   B. the *Diomedeia*
   C. the *Achaian Epic*

2. When lots were cast to find an opponent for Hector, the winner was _____
   A. Telemonian Aias
   B. Odysseus
   C. Idomeneus

3. Odysseus attempts to reconcile Achilleus by _____
   A. promising eternal fealty to the hero
   B. offering him the ship he had admired
   C. revising Agamemnon's message

4. The bad omen identified by Polydoros was _____
   A. the eagle with the serpent in its claws
   B. the raven beneath the coat of mail
   C. the albatross perched on the wall

5. Achilleus' fatal decision was to _____
   A. allow Patroklos to wear his armor
   B. defy Zeus in front of the other gods
   C. disguise himself as a Myrmidon

6. Achilleus' imminent death was prophesied by _____
   A. a horse
   B. a blind seer
   C. the weeping Briseis

7. Homer offers a symbolic episode in _____
   A. the wailing of Priam and Hekabe
   B. the battle between Achilleus and the river god
   C. Poseidon's assistance of the Argives

8. Before his classic battle with Achilleus, _____ Hektor
   A. prayed to Athene
   B. fled in fear
   C. asked his mother's blessing

9. The beginning and end of this epic poem _____
   A. shed light on Achilleus' development
   B. show the lighter side of the gods on Mount Olympos
   C. reveal Homer's concern for justice

10. The *Iliad* concludes with _____
    A. an elaborate funeral banquet
    B. the somber predictions of the gods
    C. the plans for the Trojan horse

11. Describe the use and range of similes in the *Iliad*. (See the Introduction.)

12. Describe the character of Nestor. What makes his speeches so special? (See Major Characters, Book XI, The Critics.)

13. Would you say the *Iliad* is a prowar or antiwar poem?

ANSWERS

Test 1

| 1. B | 2. B | 3. C | 4. B | 5. B | 6. C |
| 7. B | 8. B | 9. B | 10. A | | |

11. Because of a plague sent by Apollo, Agamemnon is forced to return a girl, Chryseis, he had taken as a war prize. To compensate for this loss—and the accompanying loss of

face—Agamemnon takes Achilleus' prize, Briseis, away from him. Achilleus feels this is an attack on the code of honor by which warriors fight. They take great risk to prove themselves courageous in battle, and the prizes they receive are one indication of how nobly they perform. He is also shamed at being singled out among the Achaians for this stripping and is embarrassed that it is done in front of everyone. He reasons that the war is being fought over a woman who was taken from one man by another (Paris ran away with Helen, who was married to Menelaos) and feels his situation ought to be accorded the same respect. After all, what is the value of the heroic code if it can be subverted by one man's spur-of-the-moment decision?

12. Epithets are short characteristic phrases that describe a quality or skill or position of someone. Some examples are "the lord of men" (Agamemnon); "good at the war cry" (Diomedes); and "swift-footed" (Achilleus). Epithets may be remnants of a previous oral tradition handed down intact to Homer. They are used partially to fill out the meter of the poem and sometimes are given to characters because they fit the metrical pattern of their names. They add a heroic dimension to the characters they describe, and the repetition of these qualities enlarges them over the course of the poem.

13. a. The true hero of the poem is Achilleus. He is the most important warrior, and the whole plot hinges on his anger and its consequences. Although he doesn't appear in most of the poem, his influence is felt throughout it. He is the one character actually to undergo change, and that is the theme of the *Iliad*. After he is finally made to recognize that his pride has gone too far, he tempers his anger by reaching out to Priam in peace.

b. Hektor is the hero of the *Iliad*. The noblest and purest of the characters, he fights for a cause he doesn't really believe in, because he is defending his home. He is a great warrior but also a peace-loving, domestic man, as shown by his love for his parents, wife, and children.

c. Homer believes Achilleus and Hektor are both heroes. They perform gloriously, and each represents the power of his respective army. But both are also human: Achilleus' grief transforms him and shows his emotional depth; Hektor's love of family shows his humane side.

Test 2

1. B **2.** A **3.** C **4.** A **5.** A **6.** A
7. B **8.** B **9.** A **10.** A

11. Similes are a poetic means by which Homer can take us out of the war at hand and bring in other aspects of life to expand his canvas. Often the scenes come from peaceful and domestic activities back home, reminding us of the virtues war is fighting for and providing a kind of encyclopedia of information on Greek life. Often the similes compare warriors to animals on the hunt, and this exposes the underside of brutality and inhumanness that war brings out in people. Also, similes frequently refer to natural powers like storms and tidal waves. This makes the stakes of the battles seem larger, as if two warriors fighting represented elemental battles of the universe.

12. Nestor is portrayed as the elder statesman of the Achaians. Even though he can no longer fight the way he used to, he certainly can *tell* us about the way he used to fight. His speeches are long-winded and he tends to wander a bit because of age, but his elaborate tales always have a purpose. By drawing on either his own past exploits or those of legendary heroes, he seeks to provide moral examples to his friends. The past serves as a model for present behavior.

13. a. The *Iliad* clearly shows the horror of war. On the battlefield we see mutilation of bodies graphically presented again and again. The pictures of life at Troy are filled with lamentation and grief over the fallen Trojan heroes. Great heroes on both sides die—Patroklos for the Achaians and Hektor for the Trojans. Both losses are felt strongly by Achilleus and the house of Priam, respectively. The cause of the war is not described with approval, and in the end the slaughter seems needless.

b. The *Iliad*, in spite of its graphic battle descriptions, glorifies war. Achilleus and Hektor, the greatest fighters for either side, are presented as heroes with almost divine power. They are noble warriors fighting for a code of honor, upholding their social traditions. By and large the warriors are depicted as great and glorious men, performing fantastic and heroic feats. Though they die, they die for their ideals.

Term Paper Ideas

1. What are the character differences between Achilleus and Odysseus, and what have they come to stand for in history?

2. What is the *Doloneia*?

3. Describe Homer's attitude toward the character of Paris.

4. What is the term *aristeia*, and to whom does it refer?

5. Why does Agamemnon take Briseis away from Achilleus?

6. What is the plan of Zeus, and how does it affect the poem?

7. Why do Hera and Athene support the Achaians?

8. What is the *teichoscopeia*?

9. Explain the significance of stripping a corpse of its armor. How does Homer use such an event?

10. Describe the heroic code of honor.

11. What is the *aegis*?

12. What is the significance of the scene at Troy in Book VI?

13. In terms of the plot of the *Iliad*, what happens when so many of the Achaian leaders are wounded in Book XI?

14. How does shaming operate in the *Iliad*?

15. How do we learn of domestic life other than that at Troy?

16. "Patroklos is a sacrificial victim." Explain.

17. What is the *theomachia*?

18. What is *ate*, and which characters are primarily related to it?

19. Explain the significance of the fight between Achilleus and the river Xanthos.

20. What do the funeral rites and games for Patroklos tell us about the world of the *Iliad*?

21. Do you feel Achilleus is right or wrong to be so angry at Agamemnon? Explain.

22. What relationship does Poulydamas have to Hektor?

23. Aphrodite and Helen exchange sharp words in Book III. What is the significance of their exchange?

24. What forces Achilleus finally to reenter the war?

25. Explain the significance—for Achilleus and for the poem—of Achilleus' return of Hektor's body to Priam.

Further Reading

CRITICAL WORKS

Bowra, C. M. *Tradition and Design in the "Iliad."* Oxford: Clarendon Press, 1950.

Graves, Robert. *The Greek Myths.* 2 vols. New York: Penguin Books, 1955.

Hogan, James C. *A Guide to the "Iliad."* New York: Anchor Books, 1979.

Kirk, G. S. *Homer and the Epic.* Cambridge: Cambridge University Press, 1965.

_____. *The Songs of Homer.* Cambridge: Cambridge University Press, 1962.

Murray, Gilbert. *The Rise of the Greek Epic.* Oxford: Oxford University Press, 1960.

Owen, E. T. *The Story of the "Iliad."* Ann Arbor: University of Michigan Press, 1966.

Page, Denys L. *History and the Homeric "Iliad."* Berkeley: University of California Press, 1963.

Redfield, James. *Nature and Culture in the "Iliad."* Chicago: University of Chicago Press, 1975.

Whitman, Cedric H. *Homer and the Heroic Tradition.* Cambridge, Mass.: Harvard University Press, 1958.

Wilcock, Malcolm M. *A Companion to the "Iliad."* Chicago: University of Chicago Press, 1976.

Wright, John, ed. *Essays on the "Iliad": Selected Modern Criticism.* Bloomington: Indiana University Press, 1978.

AUTHOR'S OTHER WORKS

The Odyssey
The *Homeric Hymns* are sometimes ascribed to Homer.

Glossary

Achaians One of Homer's three interchangeable terms for Greeks (also Argives, Danaans).

Achilleus Greek hero, son of Peleus and Thetis. A great warrior, possessed of fierce ideals and emotional turbulence.

Adrestos Trojan warrior taken by Menelaos and Agamemnon, but denied ransom and killed.

Aegis The powerful shield used by Athene and Zeus, derived from a thundercloud.

Agamemnon Commander-in-chief of the Greek forces, king of Mykenai.

Agenor Trojan warrior, killed by Achilleus.

Aiakides Another name for Achilleus, meaning "descendant of Aiakos."

Aiantes Plural name for the two Greek warriors named Aias.

Aias Son of Telemon (Telemonian Aias), a huge Greek warrior; also the son of Oileus, another fighter.

Aineias Major Trojan warrior. Virgil named his epic, *The Aeneid*, after him.

Alexandros Another name for Paris, Trojan prince, instigator of the war due to his capture of Helen.

Antenor Trojan elder, who urges the return of Helen.

Antilochos Son of Nestor, a Greek warrior. Figures heavily in the funeral games for Patroklos.

Aphrodite Goddess of love and beauty, guider of Helen.

Apollo Archer god, main protector of the Trojans.

Ares Furious god of war, often war itself.

Argeiphontes Another name for Hermes, who guides Priam to the Achaian camp.

Argives One of three interchangeable terms for the Greeks (also Danaans, Achaians).

Argos A Greek city, domain of Diomedes.

Aristeia The point at which a hero displays his most intense courage and valor.

Artemis Goddess of the hunt, Trojan supporter.

Askalaphos Son of Ares.

Astyanax Child of Hektor and Andromache.

Ate Moral or spiritual blindness that overtakes a character and causes ill judgment.

Athene Wise goddess of war, protectress of Achilleus and one of the main Greek supporters.

Atreides Another name for Agamemnon usually, but also for Menelaos; means "son of Atreus."

Briseis Captive girl originally awarded to Achilleus but taken by Agamemnon, precipitating the "wrath of Achilleus."

Catalog of Ships Long descriptive passage in Book II outlining all the battle contingents at Troy.

Chryseis Captive girl taken by Agamemnon. Apollo forces him to return her by sending a plague on the Greek forces.

Chryses Father of Chryseis, priest of Apollo.

Dactylic hexameter The metrical form used by Homer in his epic poems, consisting of six feet of variable quantity.

Danaans One of three interchangeable terms for the Greeks (also Argives, Achaians).

Dardanians Trojan contingent headed by Aineias.

Deception of Zeus Passage in Book XIV in which Hera seduces Zeus.

Deiphobos Brother of Hektor.

Diomedes Great Greek warrior, son of Tydeus (sometimes referred to as Tydeides). Book V is often called the *Diomedeia* because of his powerful exploits.

Dolon Trojan spy caught by Diomedes and Odysseus in Book X, which is called the *Doloneia* after him.

Epic Cycle Group of poems by various authors that make up the entire story of the Trojan War.

Epithet Short descriptive term used by Homer to describe a character, frequently repeated throughout the poem.

Eris Goddess of strife.

Eros Love-power governed by Aphrodite.

Euphorbos Trojan warrior, killed by Menelaos. His death in Book XVII is described in a famous simile.

Eurypylos Greek warrior, wounded in battle.

Glaukos Trojan warrior, ancestral friend of Diomedes, who spares his life.

Hades Ruler of the underworld, brother of Zeus and Poseidon.

Hekabe Wife of Priam, mother of Hektor.

Hektor Greatest and most beloved Trojan warrior, archenemy of Achilleus, son of Priam and Hekabe, husband of Andromache.

Helen Beautiful woman; wife of Menelaos but mistress of Paris. The Trojan War is fought on her behalf.

Helenos Trojan warrior, brother of Hektor.

Hephaistos Lame god of the blacksmith's art, creator of divine armor for Achilleus.

Hera Ever-scheming and powerful goddess; wife of Zeus, major defender of the Greek cause.

Hermes Also called Argeiphontes, god who protects Priam.

Homeric Hymns Group of narrative poems sometimes attributed to Homer.

Ichor Divine substance that runs through the immortals' veins instead of blood.

Ida Large mountain near Troy.

Idaios A herald of Priam.

Idomeneus Kretan commander, a great Greek fighter.

Ilion Another name for Troy, from which the *Iliad* gets its name.

Iris Messenger of Zeus.

Kalchas Soothsayer for the Greeks.

Kebriones Trojan warrior killed by Patroklos, sparking a fierce battle over his body.

Krete Largest of the Greek islands, whose forces are led by Idomeneus.

Kronos One of the ancient Greek gods, overthrown by Zeus, his son.

Leda Mother of Helen, perhaps by mating with Zeus in the form of a swan.

Lykaon Trojan warrior, killed by Achilleus.

Machaon Physician for the Greeks.

Medusa The "Gorgon": snake-haired creature whose severed head stared from the *aegis*.

Megaron Large Greek room.

Meleagros Legendary hero whose story is used by Phoinix to persuade Achilleus to fight.

Menelaos Ruler of Sparta, brother of Agamemnon, cuckolded husband of Helen.

Menoitios Father of Patroklos.

Meriones Greek fighter, companion of Idomeneus.

Muse One of the nine goddesses who inspire the various arts, invoked by Homer to begin the *Iliad*.

Mykenai Powerful Greek city, ruled by Agamemnon.

Myrmidons Greek contingent led by Achilleus.

Nereids Sea nymphs, companions of Thetis, daughters of Nereus.

Nestor Elder statesman of the Greeks, a great talker.

Odysseus Brilliant Greek warrior and counselor. His travels home from the war are the subject of Homer's epic, the *Odyssey*.

Oileus Father of one of the fighters called Aias.

Okeanos Primal waters surrounding the world, depicted on the divine shield of Achilleus.

Olympos Mountainous abode of the immortals.

Pandaros Trojan warrior who breaks the truce in Book IV.

Paris Another name for Alexandros, Trojan prince.

Patroklos Greek commander, comrade of Achilleus, whose death causes Achilleus to reenter the war.

Peleus Father of Achilleus.

Phoinix An elder of the Greeks, old friend of Achilleus.

Polydoros Son of Priam, killed by Achilleus.

Poseidon Fierce god of the sea and of earthquakes, brother of Zeus and Hades, defender of the Greeks.

Poulydamas Trojan warrior and friend of Hektor.

Priam King of Troy, father of Hektor and many others.

Pylos Greek city, domain of Nestor.

Rhapsode Ancient Greek singer who recited epics.

Rhesos Trojan ally, killed by Diomedes; possessor of great horses.

Sarpedon Son of Zeus, a Trojan fighter whose death almost causes Zeus to intervene.

Skaian Gates Landmark gates before the walls of Troy.

Skamandros River that crosses the plain of Troy (also called the plain of Skamandros). Also referred to as Xanthos.

Sparta Greek city, home of Menelaos.

Teichoscopeia "View from the wall": referring to Helen's description of the Greek forces as seen from the Trojan walls.

Telemon Father of one of the Greek fighters called Aias.

Teukros Younger brother of Telemonian Aias, a great archer.

Theomachia "Battle of the gods": referring to the immortals' fight in Book XXI.

Thersites Offensive Greek fighter; a buffoon and a whiner.

Thetis Sea goddess, mother of Achilleus.

Troy Walled city on the coast of Turkey; also called Ilion.

Tydeus Father of Diomedes; sometimes referred to as Tydeides.

Tyndareus Father, perhaps, of Helen.

Xanthos Another name for the river Skamandros.

Zeus Most powerful of the immortals, a thunder-and-lightning sky god. His plan outlines the plot of the *Iliad*.

The Critics

On Achilleus

The *Iliad* traces almost clinically the stages of Achilles' development. More than tragedy, epic makes real use of time; whereas Oedipus, for instance, reveals himself before our eyes, Achilles creates himself in the course of the poem. He progresses from young hopefulness, cheerfully accepting the possibility of early death with glory, through various phases of disillusion, horror, and violence, to a final detachment which is godlike indeed. Tragedy, especially that of Sophocles, slowly uncovers a character which is complete from start to finish, but Achilles is actually not complete until the poem is complete. He is learning all the time.

—*Cedric H. Whitman*, Homer and the Heroic Tradition, *1958*

On Similes

The similes have a double purpose: to crystallize, in a sphere close to the listener's own understanding, a sight or sound or a state of mind; and to give relief from the harshness and potential monotony of warfare by suddenly actualizing a quite different and often even peaceful, even domestic, scene. . . .

—*G. S. Kirk*, The Songs of Homer, *1962*

On Hektor

Hector is the pure patriot, who is fighting to save his city, not to defend his brother's guilt; he feels the sin of Paris as a stain upon his city's name, a fatal weakness in the Trojan cause. Thus he enters the poem with his nobility and purity of motive thrown into sharp relief against the background of guilt which spells Troy's inevitable destruction.

—*E. T. Owen*, The Story of the "Iliad," *1966*

On Nestor

Nestor's constant claim is that he has lived a hero's life. Having already proved his worth in heroic encounters, he sets his life before the young heroes as paradigm. Now it is their turn to prove their characters. As paradigms, then, his stories are never told for their antiquarian interest but because they are his most persuasive form of rhetoric. . . . They reflect a pervasive need to justify an action in the present by an appeal to a past precedent.

—*Norman Austin, "The Function of Digressions in the* Iliad," *in John Wright*, Essays on the "Iliad," *1978*

On Greatness

Achilles' greatness is a greatness of force and negation. He is different from other men by his greater capacity to deny, to refuse, to kill, and to face death. . . . Hector, by contrast, is a hero of illusions; he is finally trapped between a failed illusion and his own capacity for disillusionment. Hector is surely a figure less grand than Achilles, but it is Hector's story that gives Achilles' story meaning; Hector affirms all that Achilles denies.

—*James Redfield*, Nature and Culture in the "Iliad," *1975*